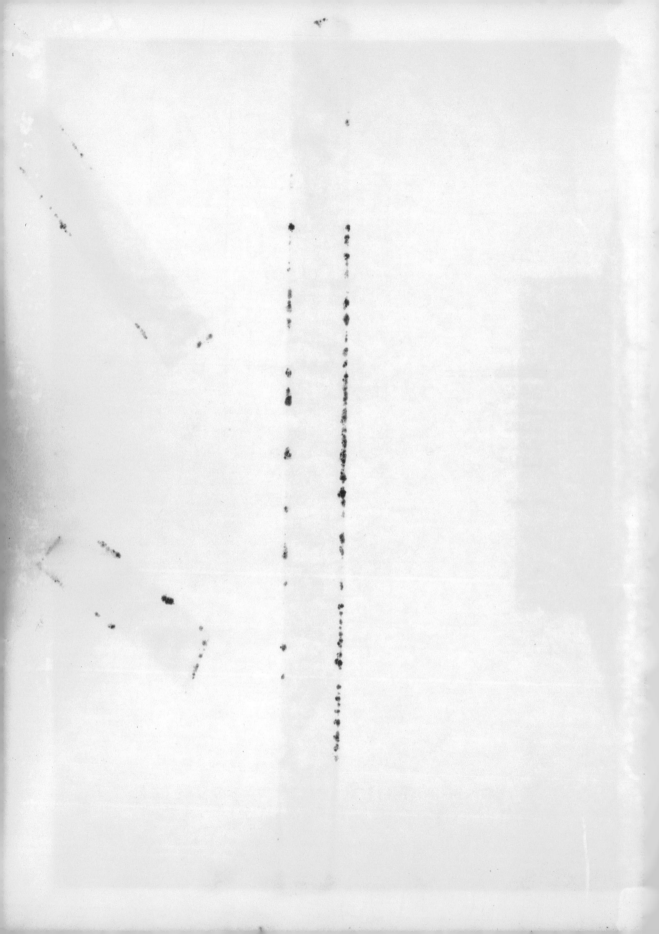

ROAD ATLAS

OF GREAT BRITAIN

FIFTH-INCH TO MILE

15th Edition

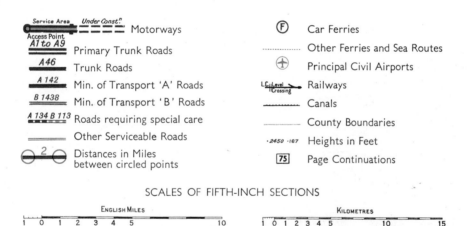

Service Area / Under Const.? ▬▬═ ═ ═ ═ Motorways

Access Point / A1 to A9 Primary Trunk Roads

A46 Trunk Roads

A 142 Min. of Transport 'A' Roads

B 1438 Min. of Transport 'B' Roads

A 134 B 113 Roads requiring special care

Other Serviceable Roads

2 Distances in Miles between circled points

Ⓕ Car Ferries

Other Ferries and Sea Routes

✈ Principal Civil Airports

L.C. Level Crossing Railways

Canals

County Boundaries

·2450 ·167 Heights in Feet

75 Page Continuations

SCALES OF FIFTH-INCH SECTIONS

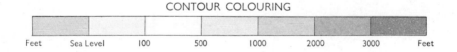

ENGLISH MILES
1 0 1 2 3 4 5 10

KILOMETRES
1 0 1 2 3 4 5 10 15

As an aid to measuring distances, borders of Fifth-Inch Sections are divided into One-Mile units, the Town Plans into Quarter-Mile units and the Tenth-Inch Maps into Two-Mile units

CONTOUR COLOURING

| Feet | Sea Level | 100 | 500 | 1000 | 2000 | 3000 | Feet |

Printed and Published in Great Britain

© **JOHN BARTHOLOMEW & SON LTD.**

12 Duncan Street, Edinburgh 9

1962

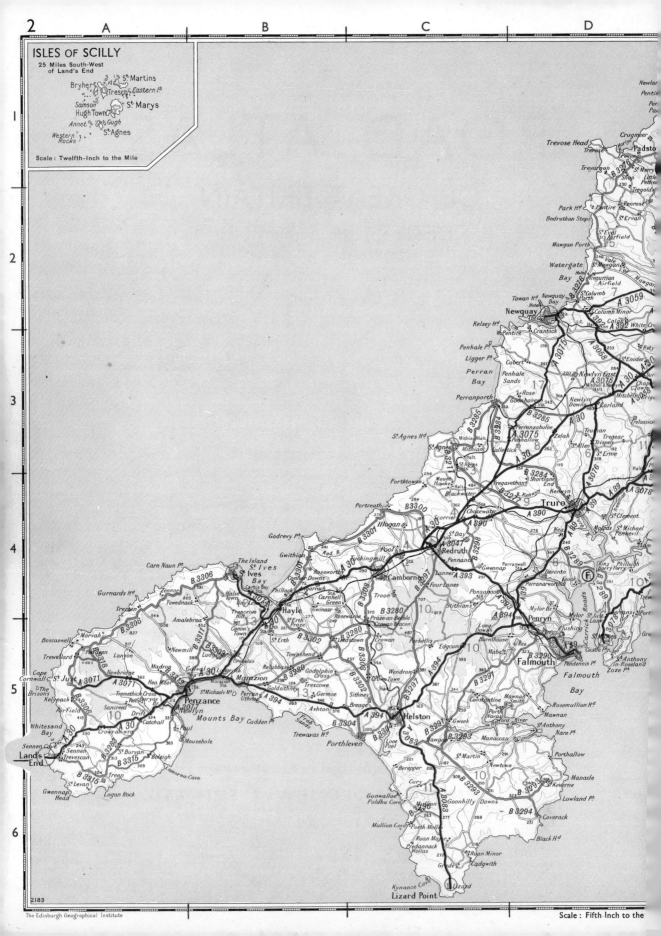

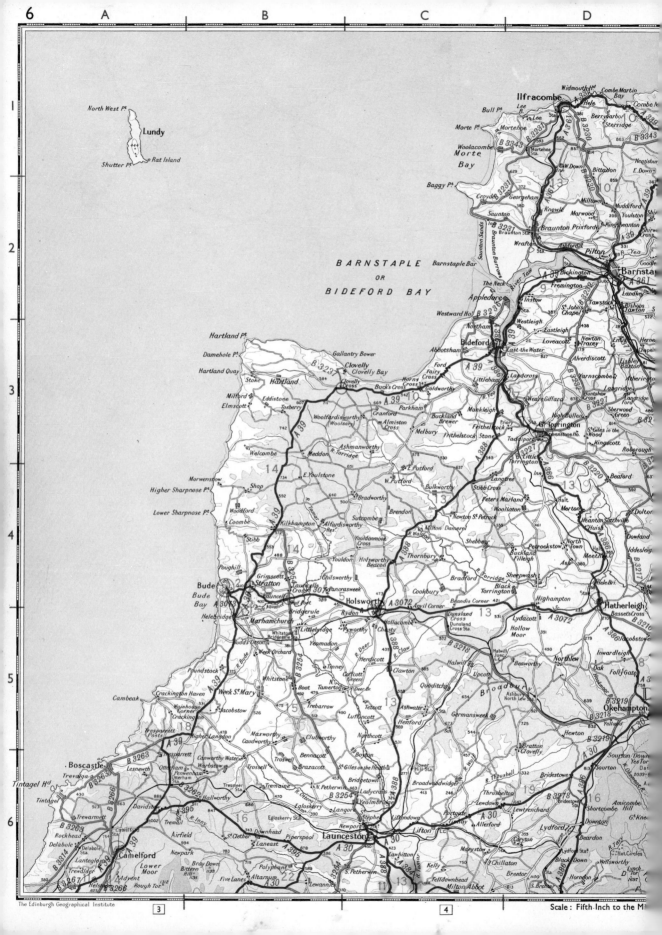

A   **B**   **C**   **D**

BARNSTAPLE
OR
BIDEFORD BAY

Lundy
North West Pt
Rat Island
Shutter Pt

Ilfracombe
Combe Martin Bay
Widmouth Hd
Bull Pt
Lee
Hele
Berrynarbor
Sterridge
Morte Pt
Mortehoe
Woolacombe
Morte Bay
W. Down
Bittadon
E. Down
Baggy Pt
Croyde
Georgeham
Knowl
Marwood
Muddiford
Youlston
Saunton
Braunton
Prixford
Kingsheanton
Wrafton
Ashford
Pilton
Barnstaple
Appledore
The Neck
Instow
Bickington
Fremington
Westward Ho!
Northam
Westleigh
St John's Chapel
Tawstock
Bishops Tawton
Bideford
East-the-Water
Eastleigh
Loveacott
Newton Tracey
Alverdiscott
Fishley Barton
Abbotsham
Ford
Fairy Cross
Littleham
Landcross
Yarnscombe
Langridge

Hartland Pt
Damehole Pt
Hartland Quay
Gallantry Bower
Clovelly
Clovelly Bay
Horns Cross
Buck's Cross
Goldworthy
Gt. Torrington
Stevenstone Ho.
Giles in the Wood
Kingscott
Roborough
Stoke
Hartland
Milford
Elmscott
Eddistone
Tosberry
Woolfardisworthy
(Woolsery)
Cranford
Almiston Cross
Parkham
Melbury
Buckland Brewer
Frithelstock
Frithelstock Stone
Taddiport
Little Torrington
Beaford
Welcombe
Meddon
Ashmansworthy
R. Torridge
Langtree
Stibb Cross
Peters Marland
Woollaton
Merton
Heanton Satchville
Huish
Dowland
Shop
E. Youlstone
E. Putford
W. Putford
Bulkworthy
Newton St Petrock
Morwenstow
Higher Sharpnose Pt
Lower Sharpnose Pt
Woodford
Coombe
Stibb
Poughill
Welcombe
Kilkhampton
Alfardisworthy
Res.
Sutcombe
Brendon
Milton Damerel
Shebbear
Buckland Filleigh
North Town
Ash
Iddesleigh
Bradworthy
Youldonmoor Cross
Youldon
Holsworthy Beacon
R. Waldon
Thornbury
Petrockstow
Meeth
Chilsworthy
Bradford
R. Torridge
Sheepwash
Black Torrington
Highampton
Hatherleigh
Bassets Cross
Bude
Bude Bay
Stratton
Launceston Cross
Pancrasweek
Holsworthy
Hollacombe
Cookbury
Beandis Corner
Lydacott
Hollow Moor
Jacobstowe
Helebridge
Marhamchurch
Bridgerule
Rydon
Pyworthy
Chasty
Dunsland Cross
Northlew
Inwardleigh
Oak
Folly Gate
Whitstone Bridgerule Sta.
Littlebridge
Yeomadon
R. Deer
Herdicott
R. Claw
Halwill Junc.
Halwill
Upcott
Budd's Titson
Week Orchard
Tinney
Coffcott Green
Deer Pk.
Clawton
Ashwater
Ashbury
North Lew
Germansweek
Beaworthy
Bratton Clovelly
Poundstock
Whitstone
Boot
Tamerton
Trebarrow
Luffincott
Tettcott
Henford
Broadbury
Hewton
Okehampton
Sourton Down
Cambeak
Crackington Haven
Week St Mary
Jacobstow
Maxworthy
Clubworthy
Northcott
Quoditch
Boyton
Boscastle
Tresparrett Posts
Higher Langdon
Caudworthy
Bennacott
Troswell
Brazacott
St Giles on the Heath
Bridgetown
Broadwoodwidger
Bratton Clovelly
Sourton
Bridestowe
Tintagel Hd
Tresparrett
Lesnewth
Otterham
Warbstow
Trewassa
Tremaine
N. Petherwin
Ladycross
Portgate
Lewdown
Lewtrenchard
Amicombe Hill
Shortcombe
Tintagel
Trevalga
Davidstow
Hallworthy
Tresmeer
Eglarooke
Langore
St Stephen
Lifton
Lydford
Beardon
Rockhead
Delabole
Trewarmett
Tremail
Tremail
St Clether
Downhead
Laneast
Newport
Launceston
Lifton
Lifton Down
Carey
Chillaton
Camelford
Lower Moor
Airfield
Newpark
Bray Down
Bittern Hills
Polyphant
Lewannick
S. Petherwin
Lawhitton
Kelly
Brentor
Adgent
Rough Tor
Five Lanes
Altarnun
Felldownhead
Milton Abbot

A 39   B 3231   B 3230   A 361   A 39   A 386   A 388   A 3072   A 30   A 395   A 3079   B 3254   B 3262   B 3263   B 3264   B 3266   B 3267   B 3268

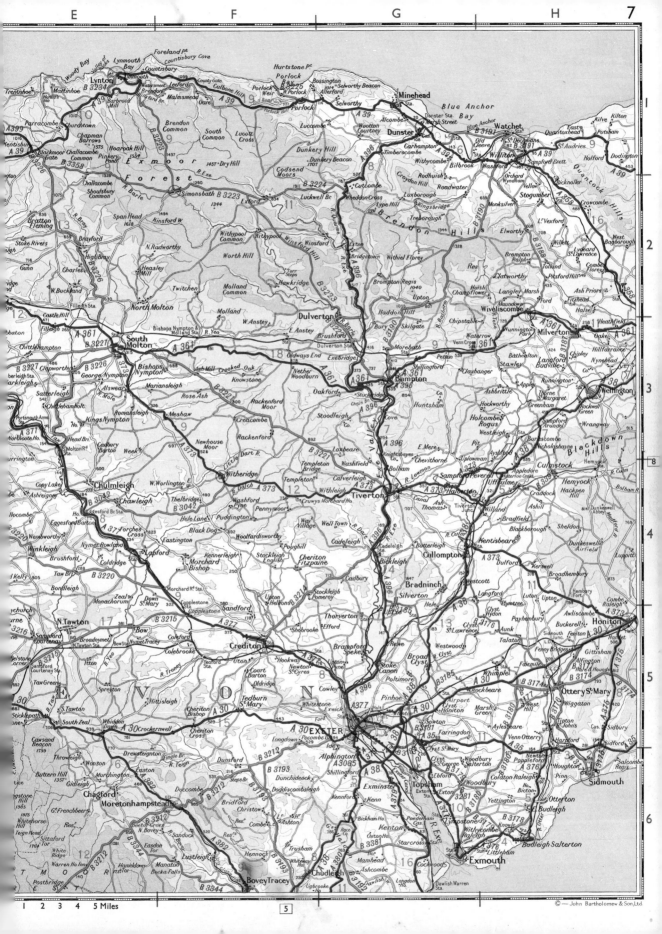

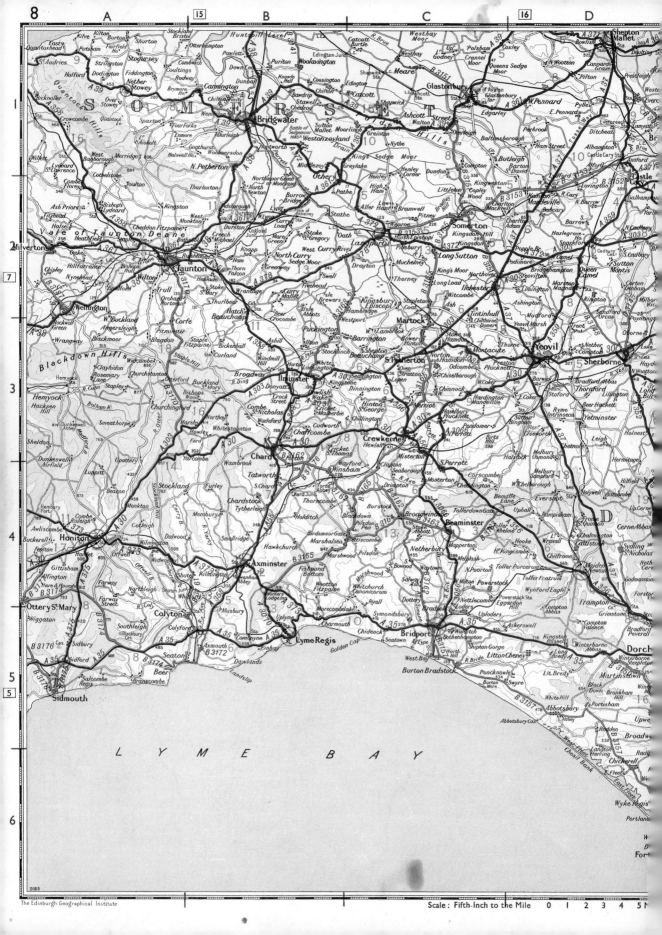

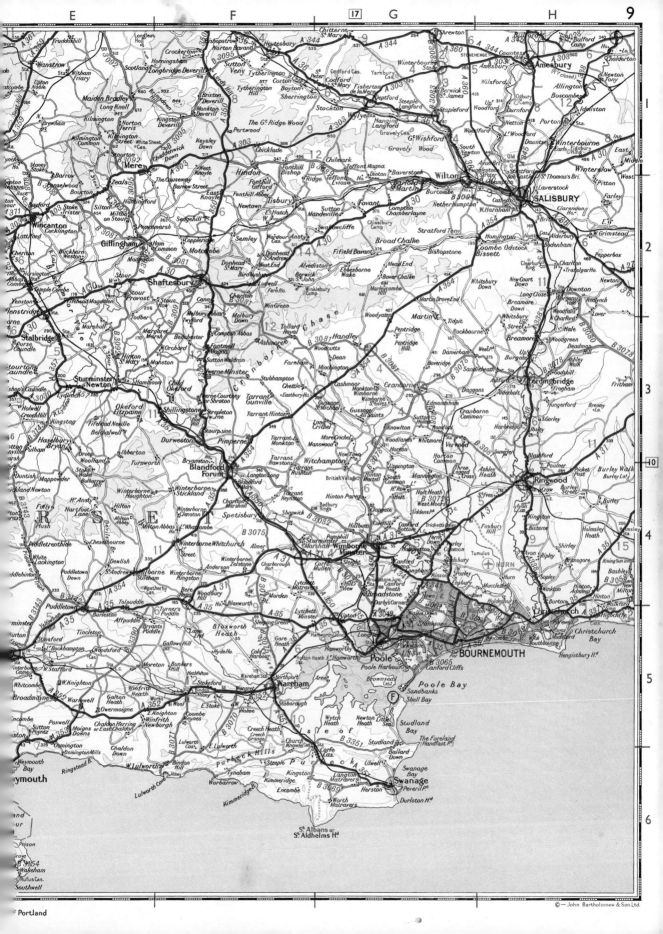

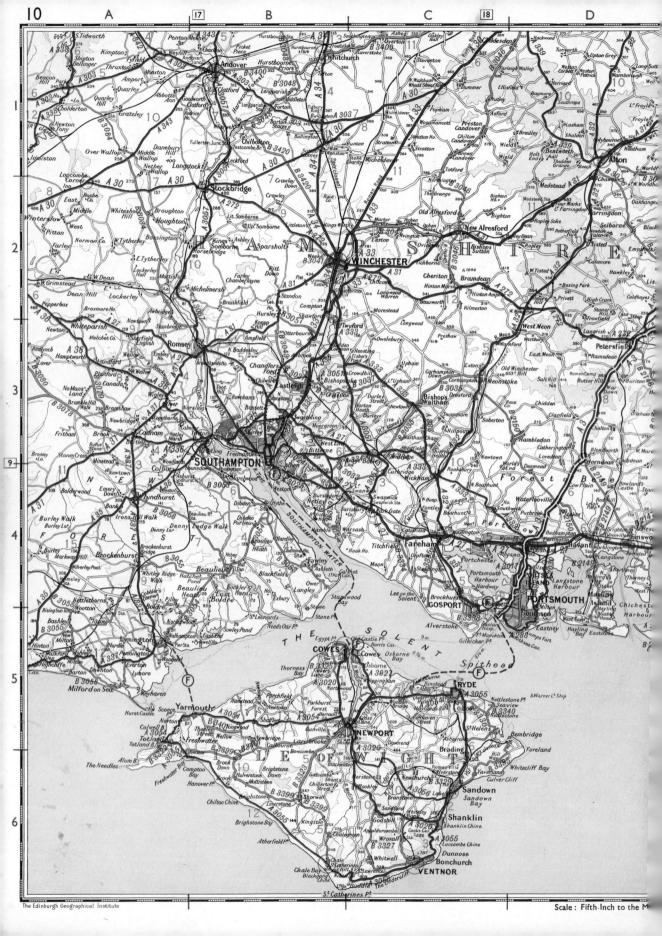

Scale : Fifth-Inch to the M

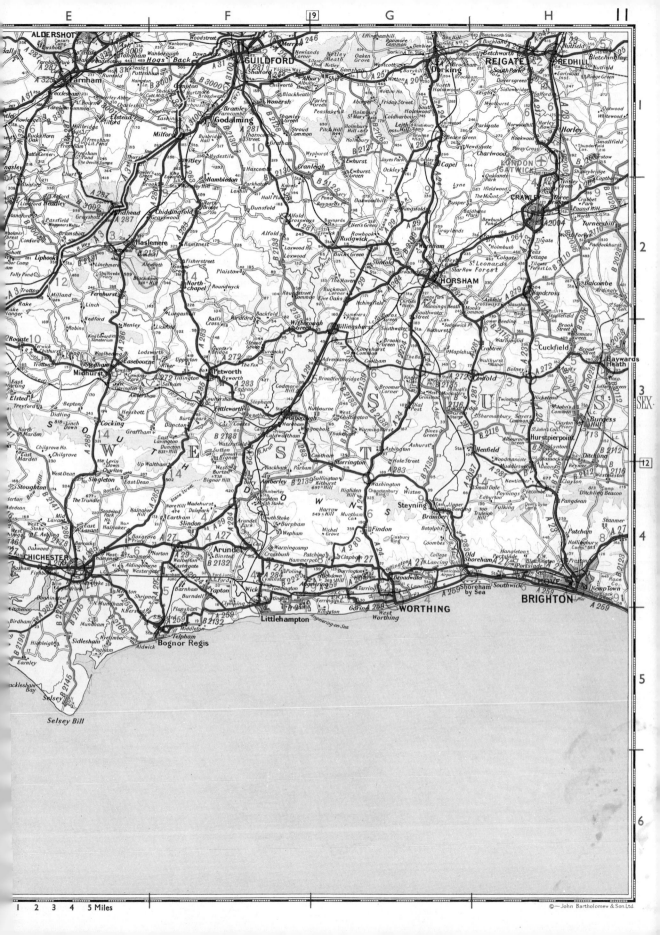

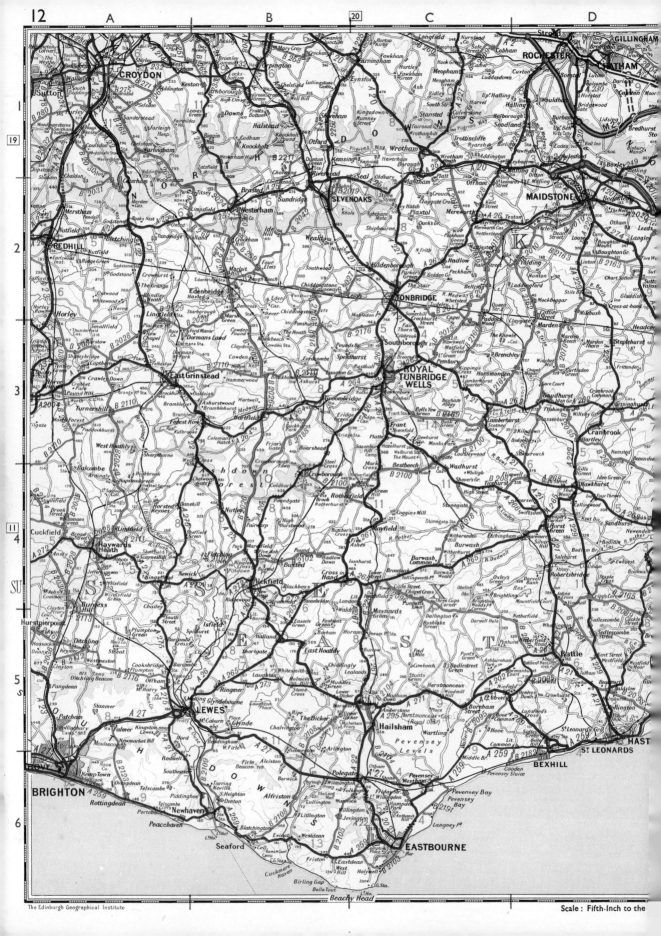

Scale : Fifth-Inch to the

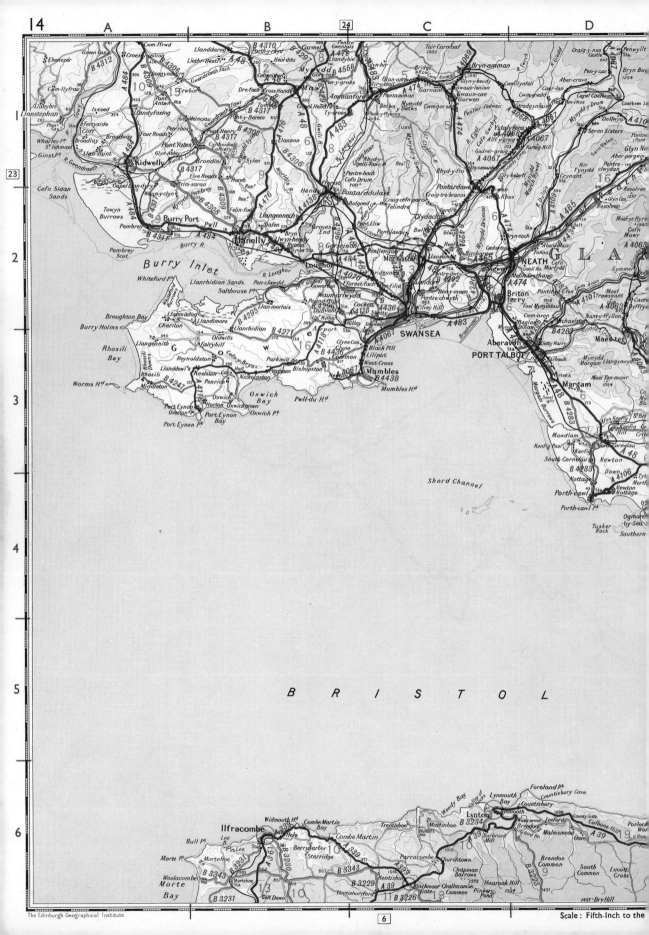

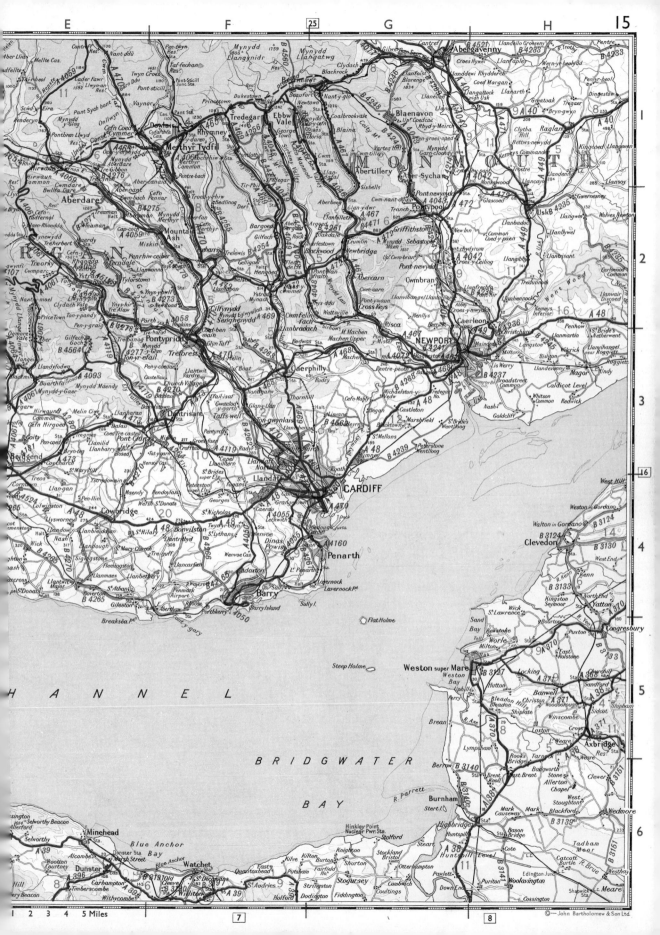

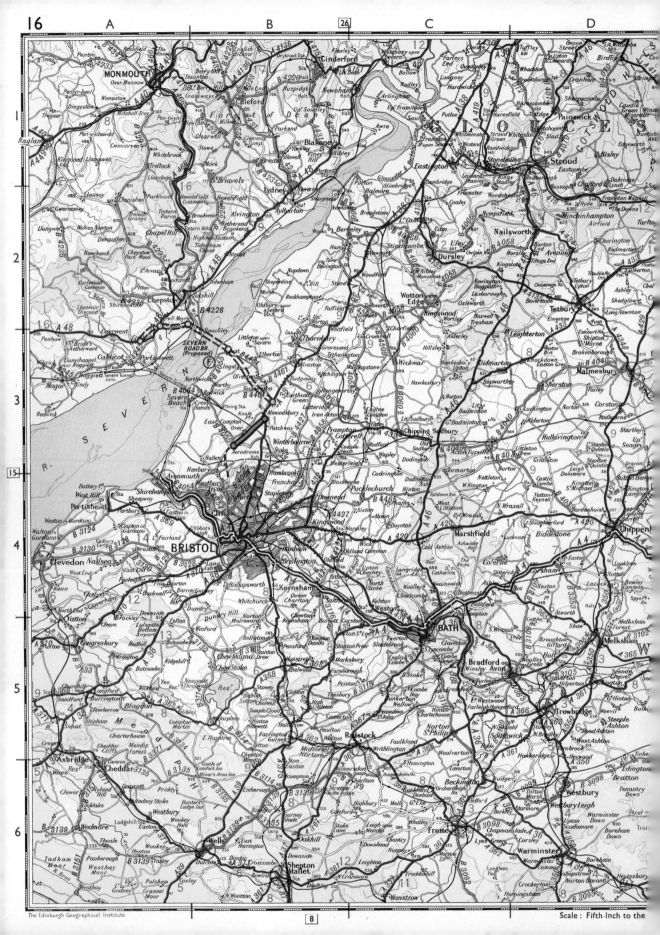

Scale: Fifth-Inch to the

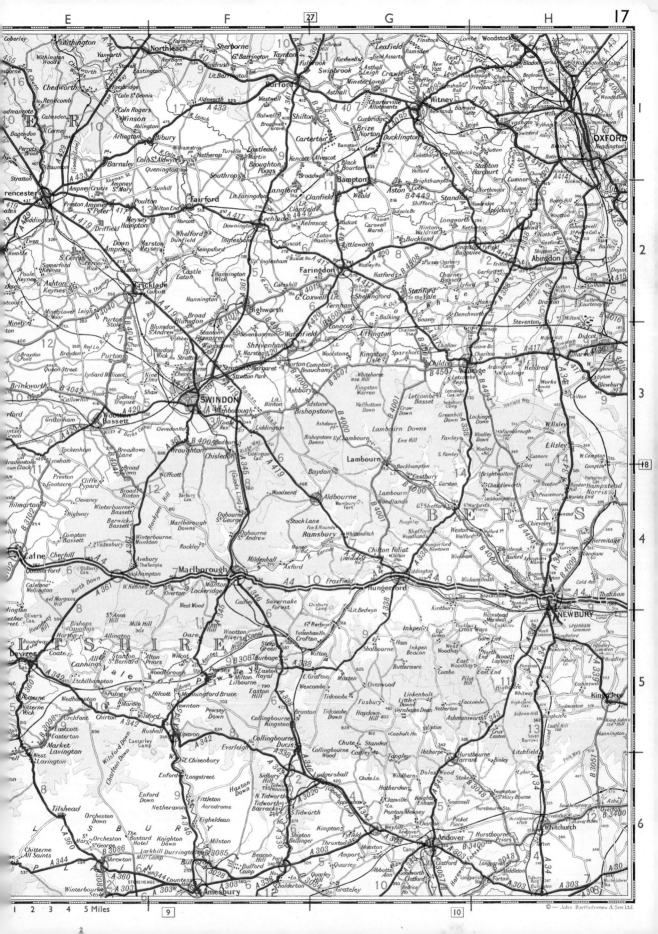

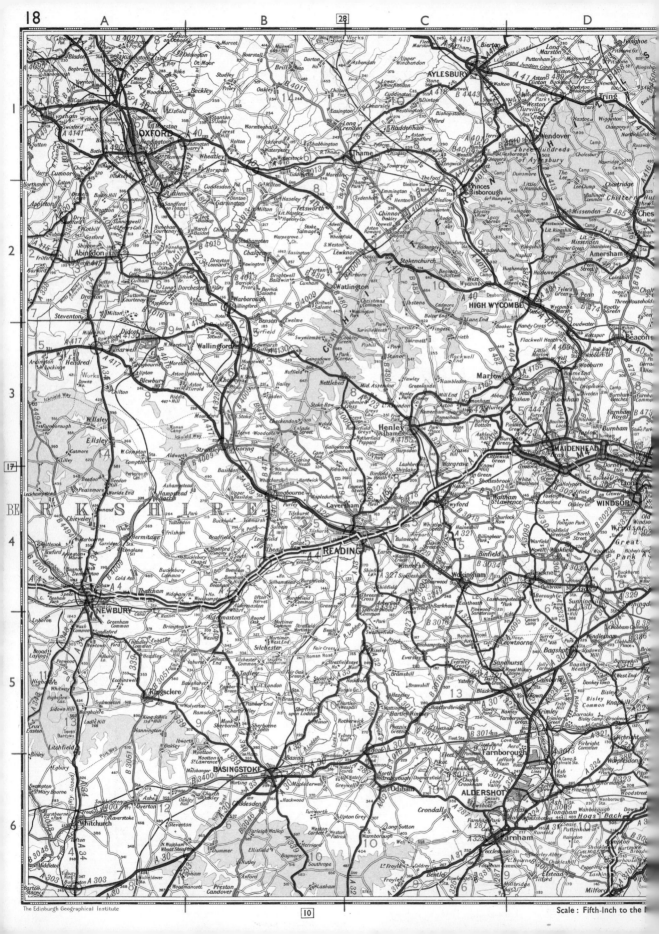

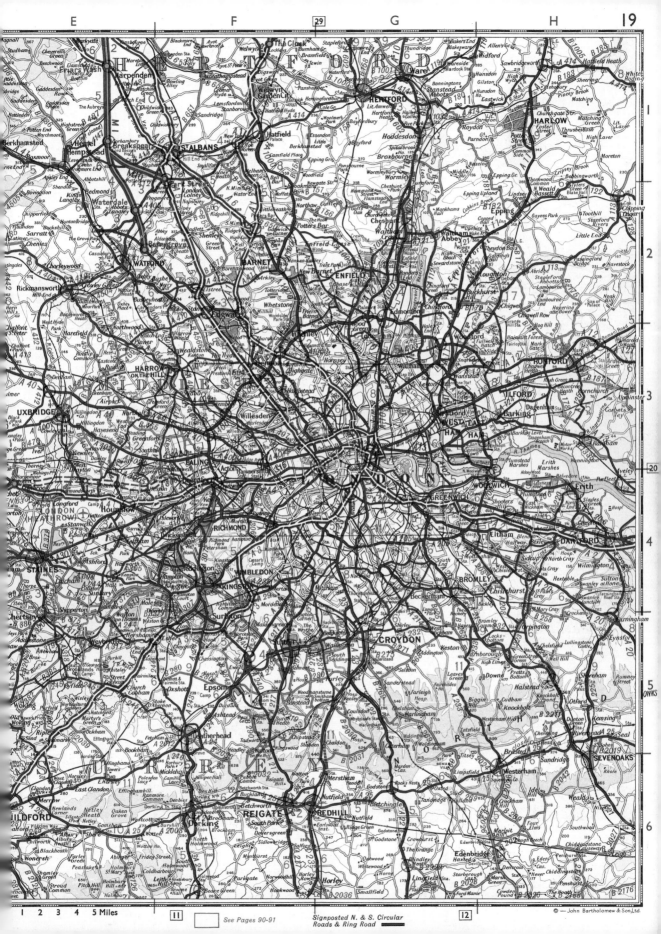

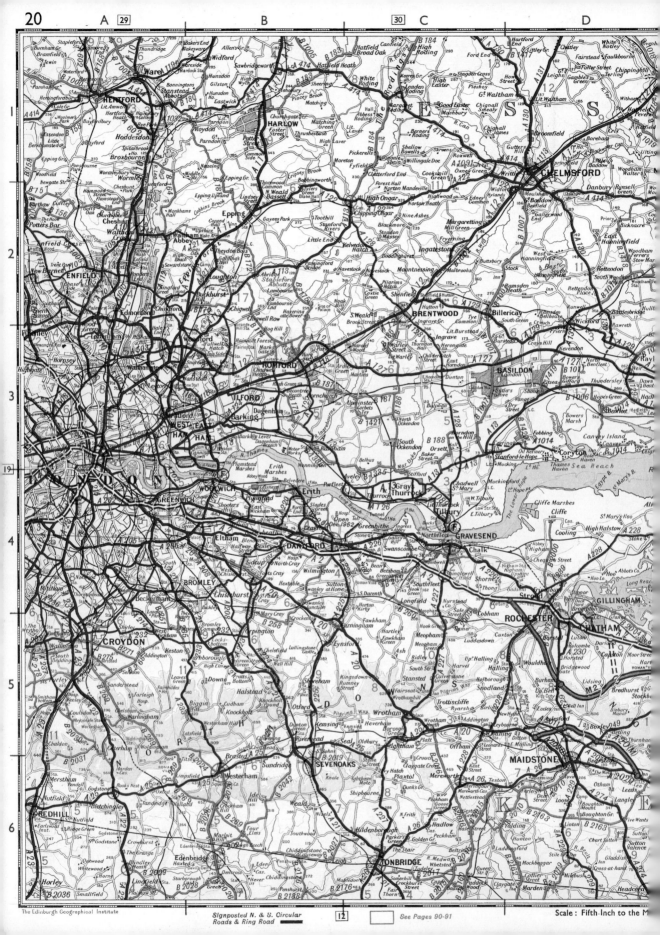

Signposted N. & S. Circular
Roads & Ring Road

12

See Pages 90-91

Scale : Fifth-Inch to the M

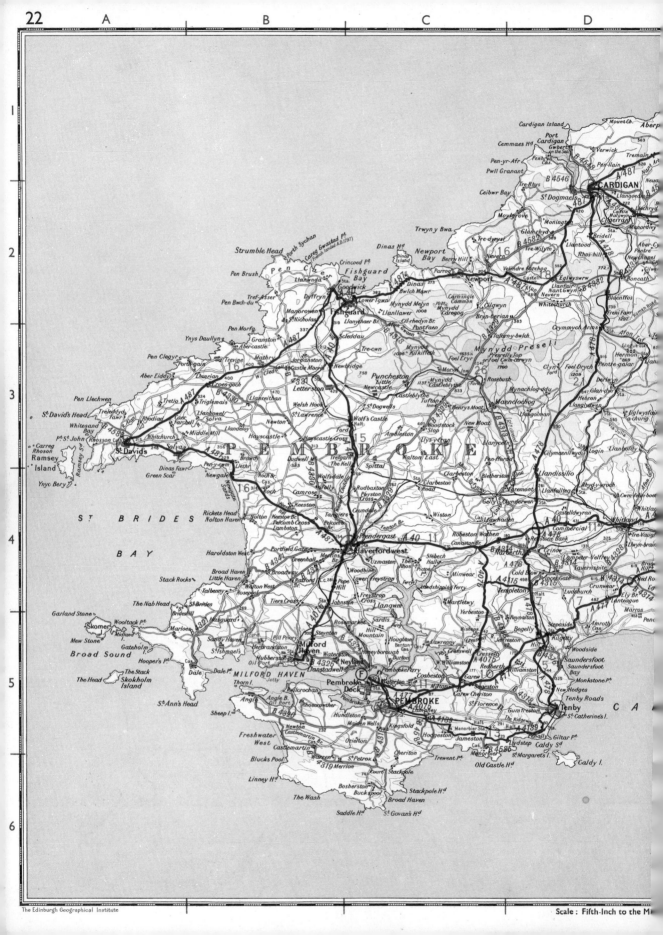

A   B   C   D

1

2

3

4

5

6

P E M B R O K E

St BRIDES BAY

Broad Sound

MILFORD HAVEN

CARDIGAN

Fishguard

Haverfordwest

St Davids

Pembroke

Tenby

Newport

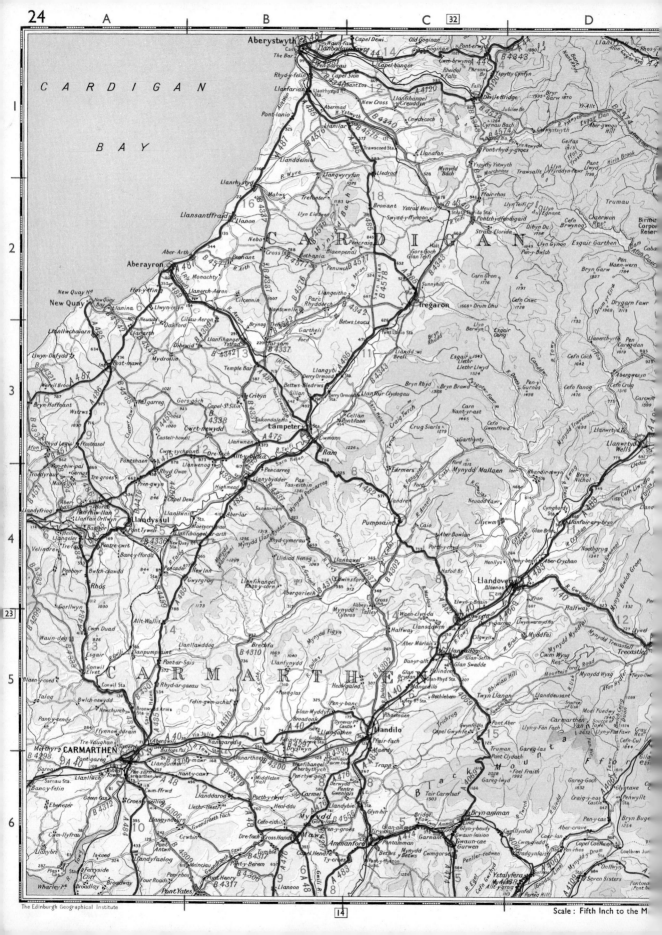

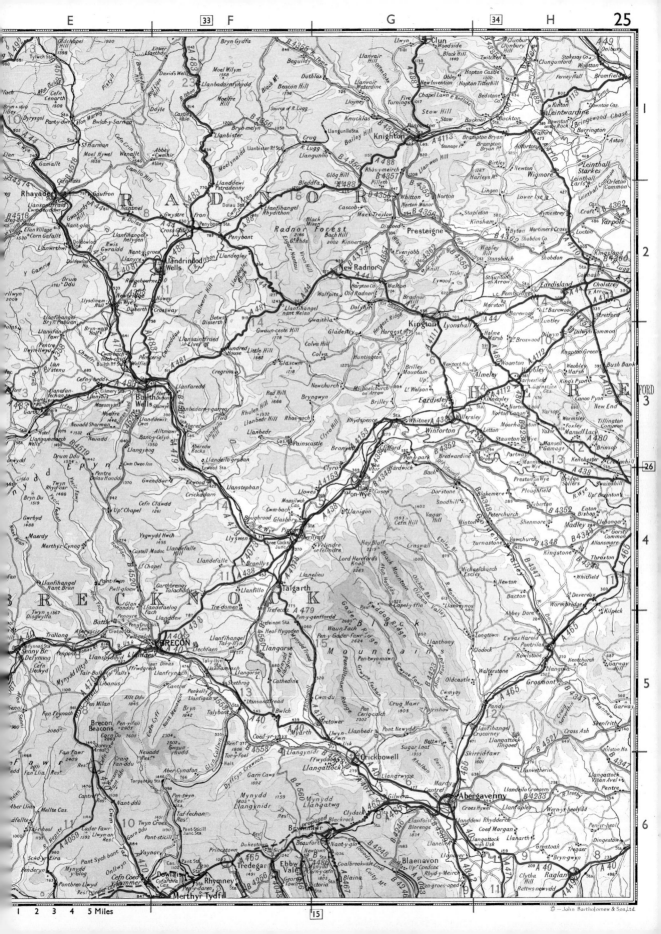

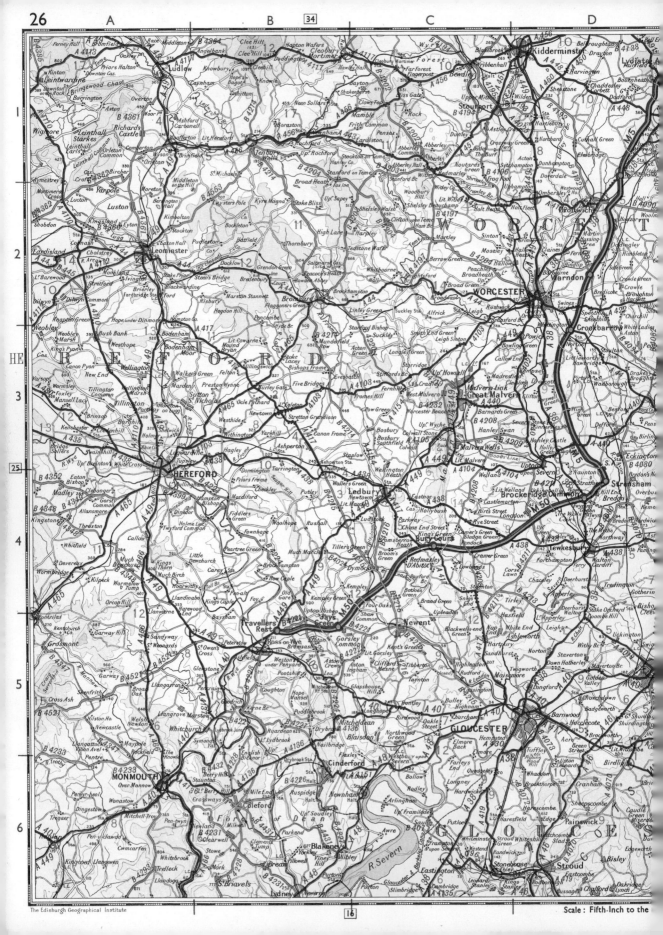

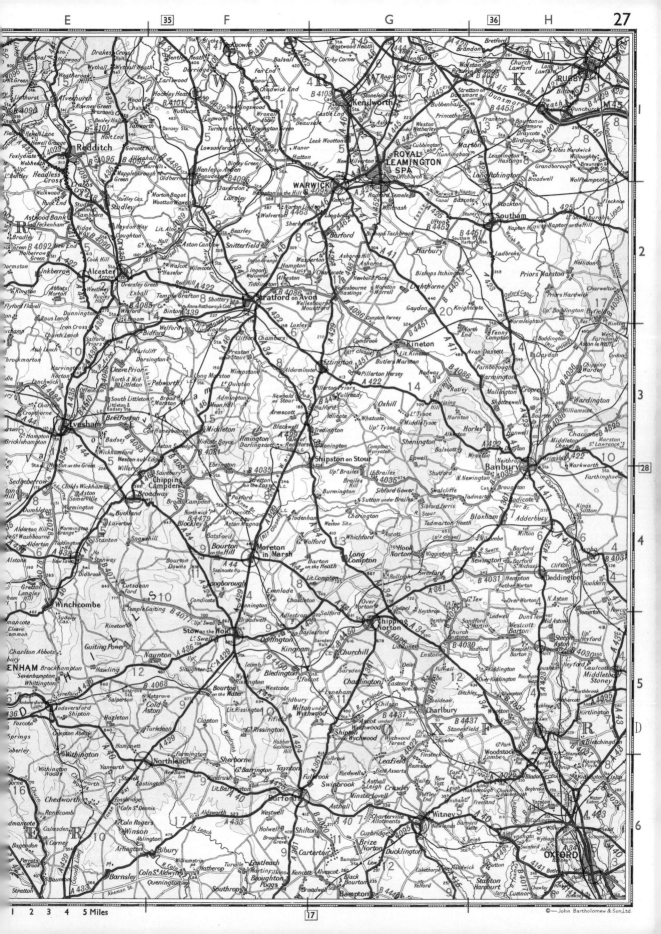

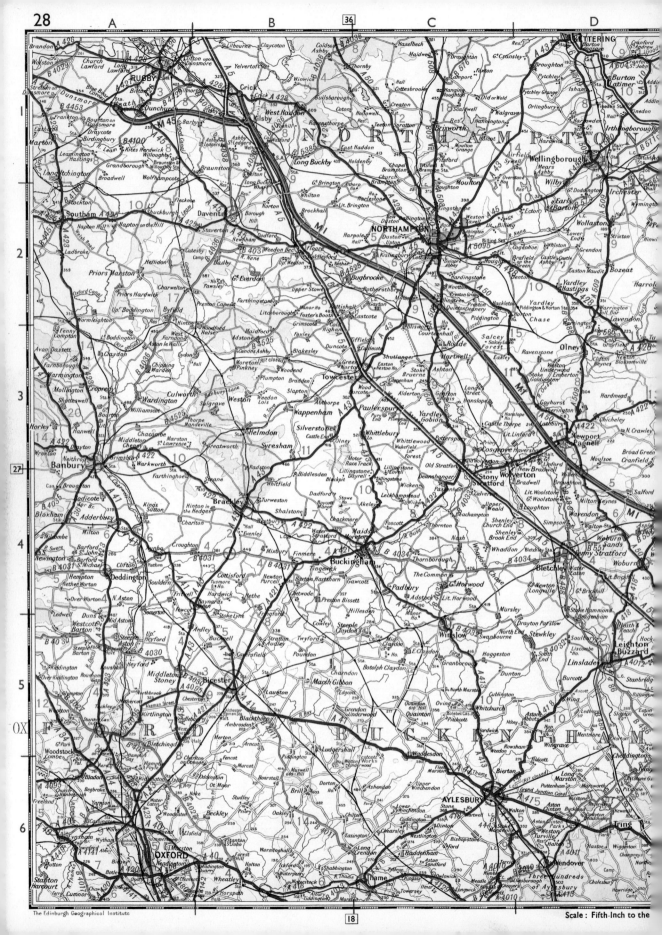

Scale : Fifth-Inch to the

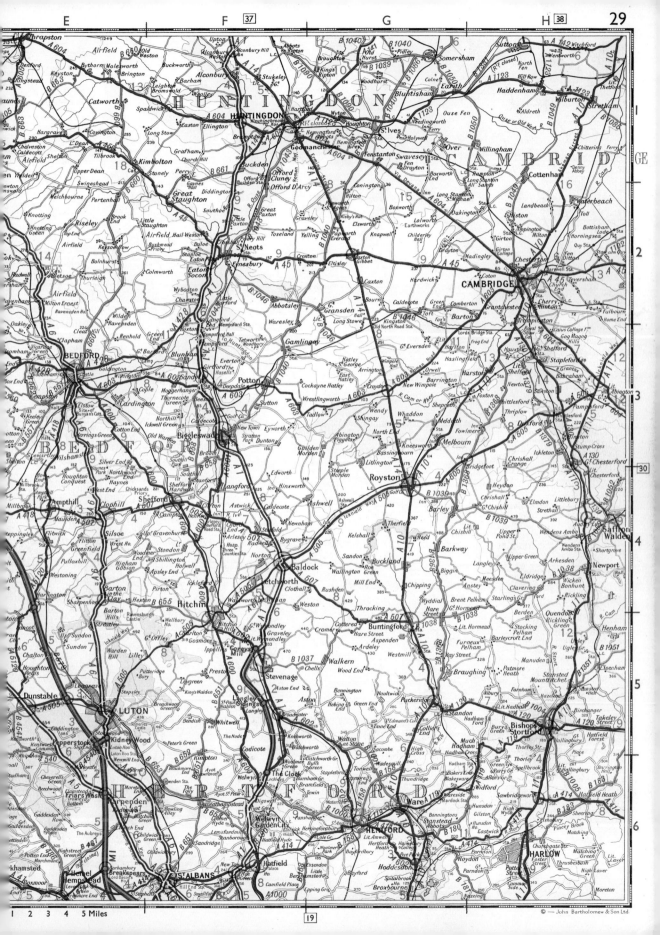

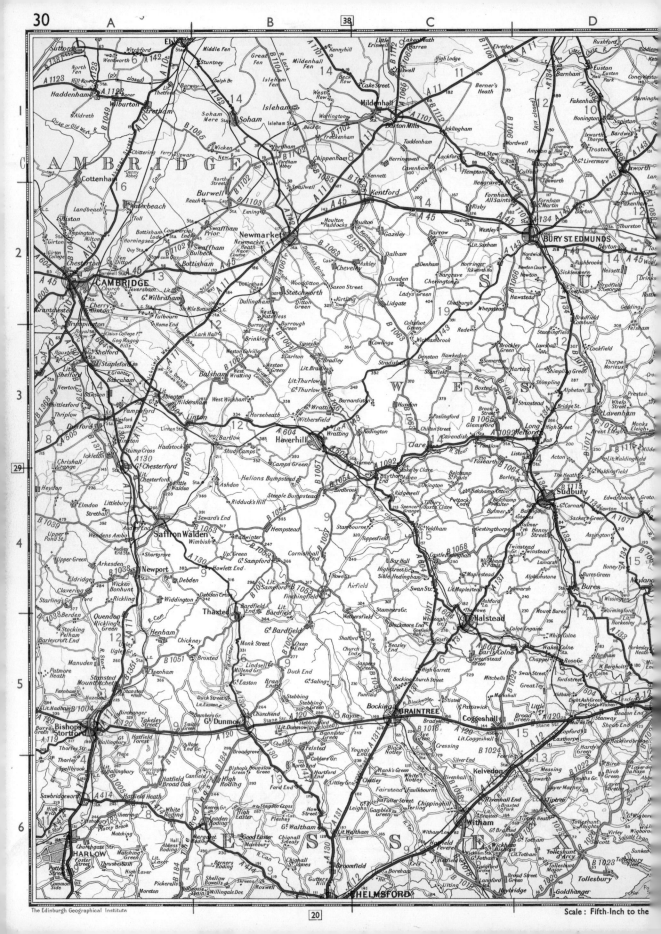

Scale: Fifth-Inch to the

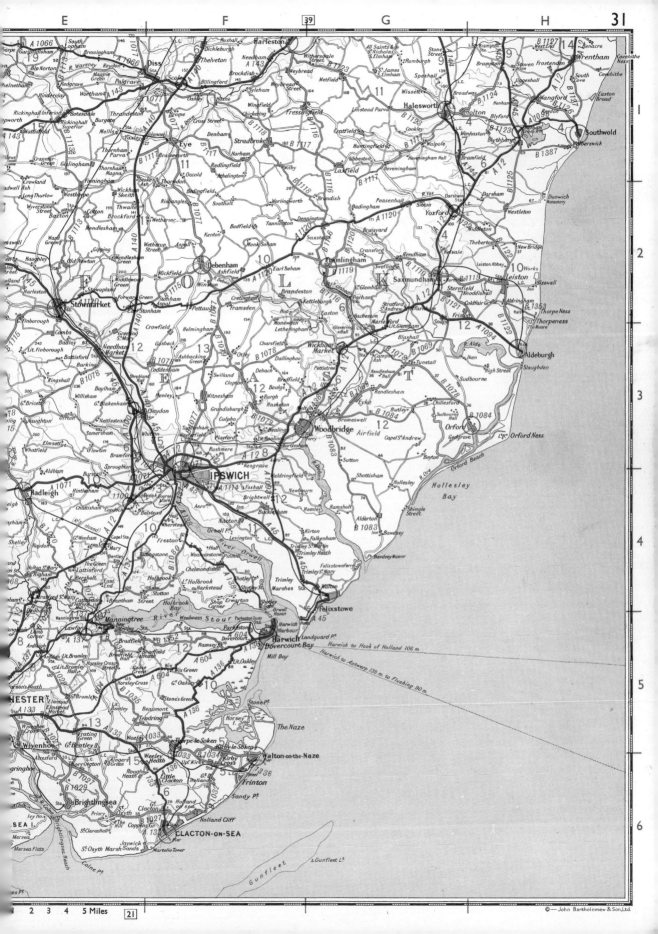

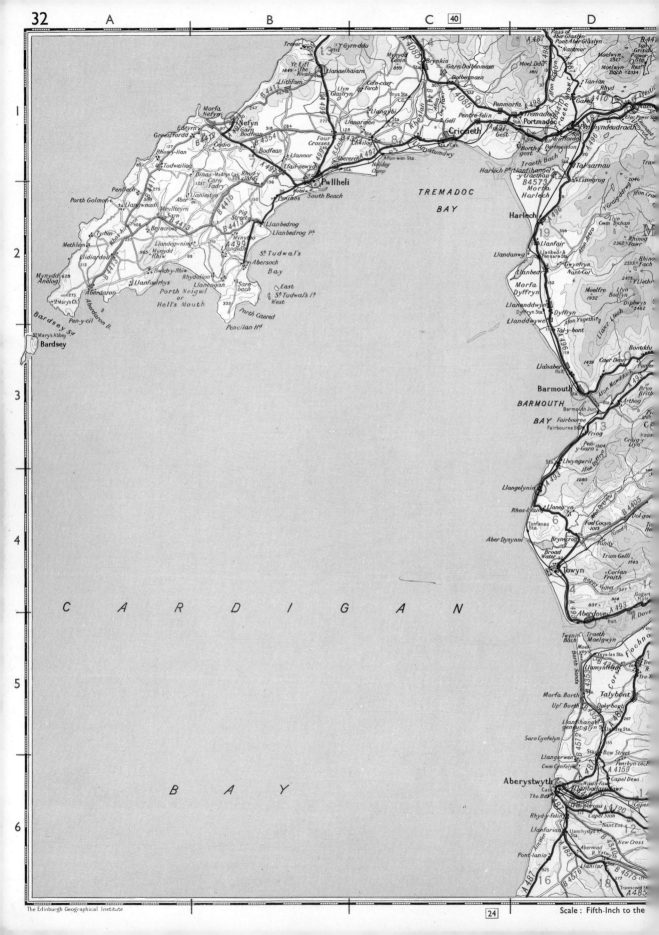

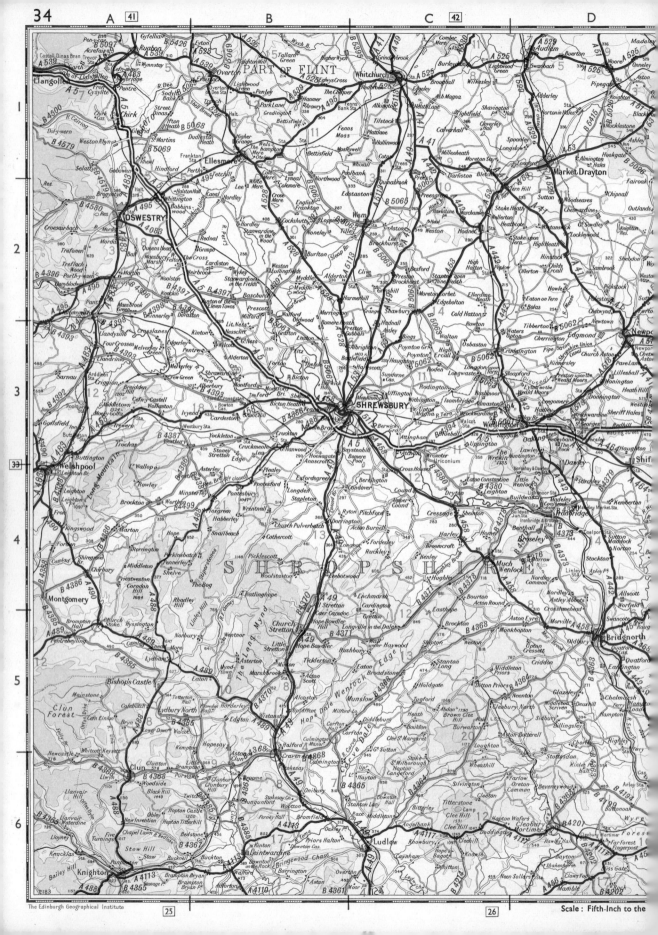

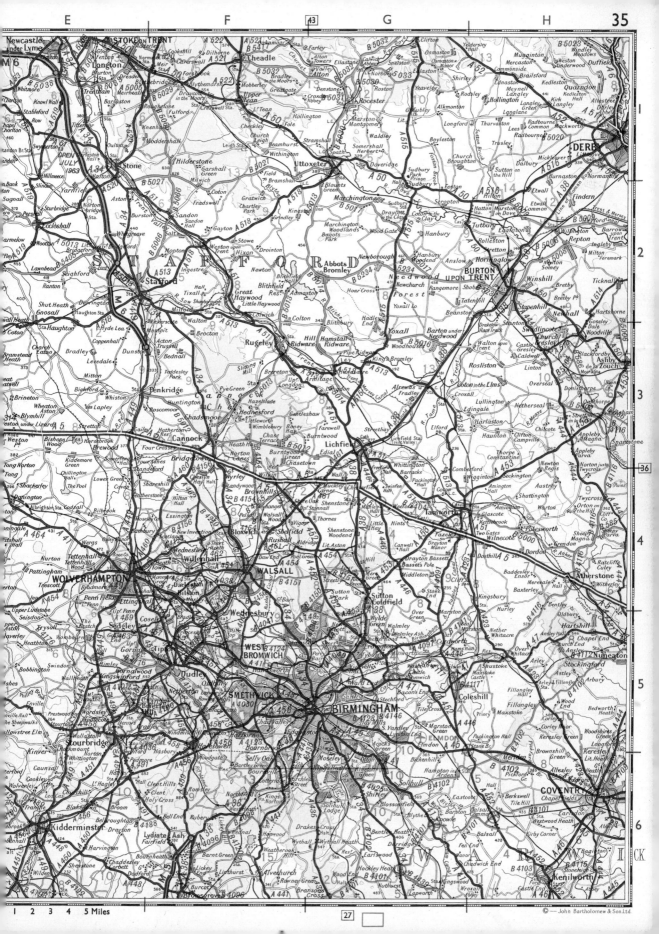

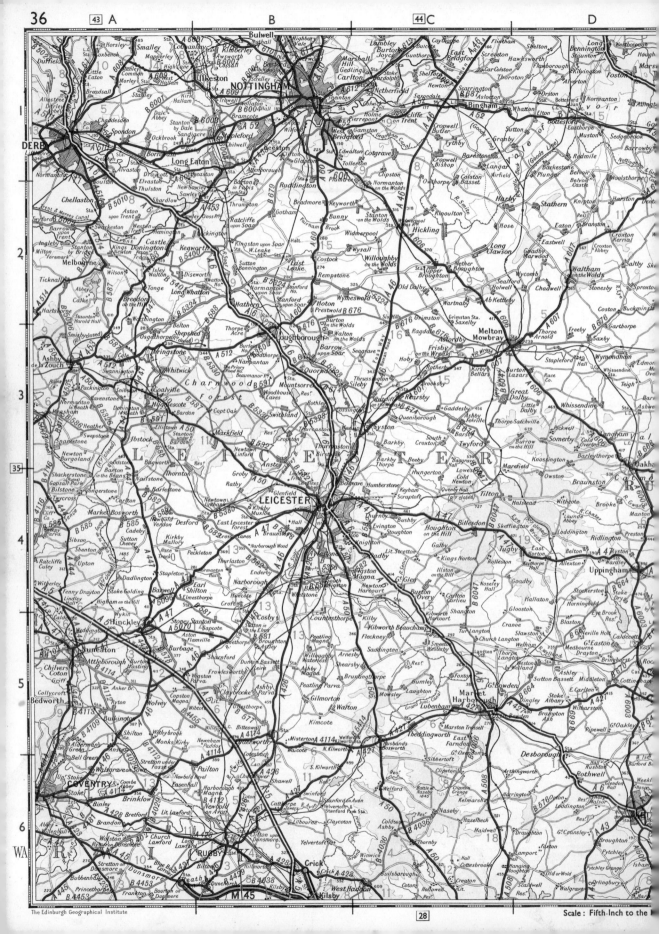

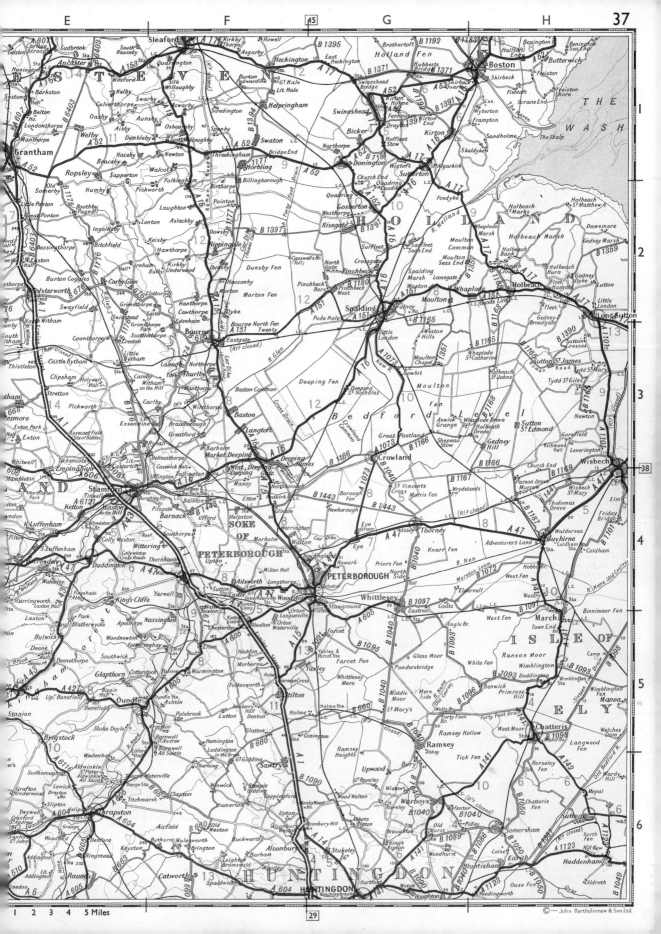

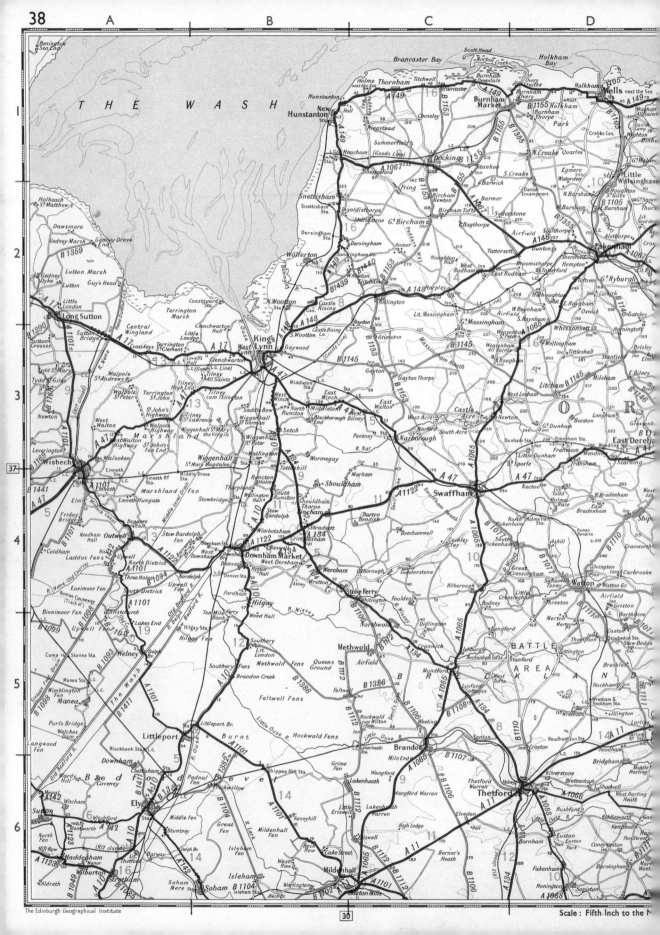

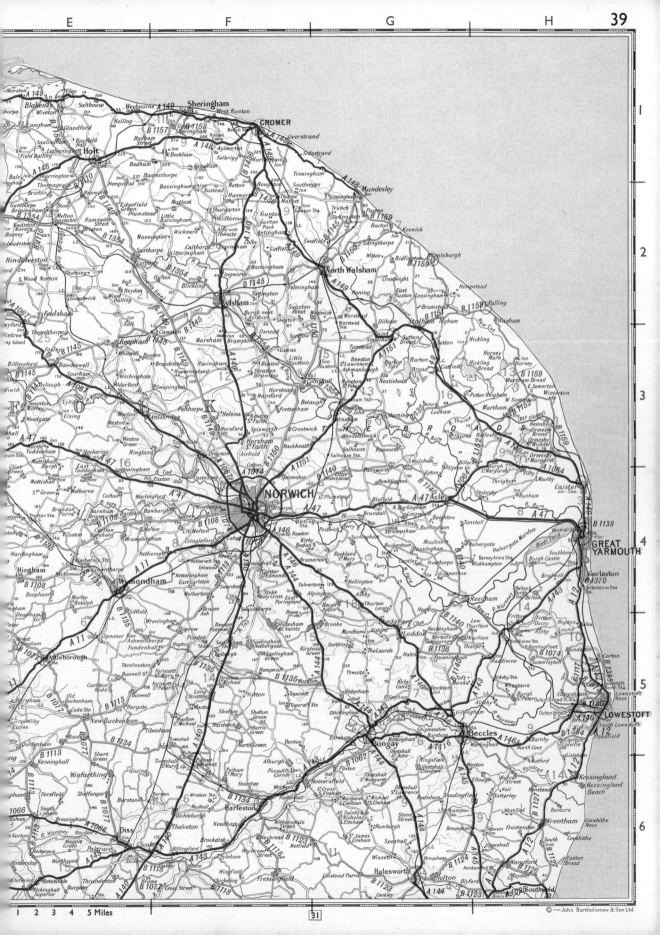

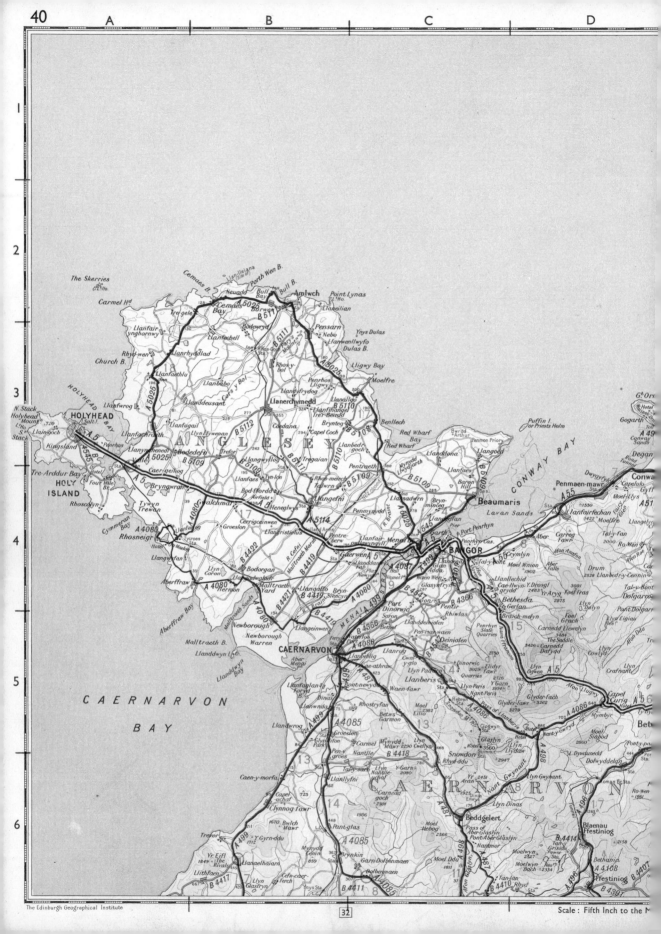

A   B   C   D

1

2

The Skerries

Carmel Hd

Cemaes B. Porth Wen B.

Llanllwna Bull B.

Neuadd Bull Bay Amlwch

Cemaes 5025 Burwen Point Lynas

Tre gele Cemaes B 511 Bay Llaneilian

Llanfair Bodewryd Pensarn

ynghornwy Nebo

Llanfechell B 6111 Llanwenllwyfo Dulas B.

Rhyd wen Parys Mount Ynys Dulas

Church B. Llanrhyddlad Rhos-goch A 5025 Lligwy Bay

3

HOLYHEAD Llanfaethlu Rhos-y-bol Moelfre

N. Stack Llanbabo Penrhos Lligwy

Holyhead Llanddeusant Cors y Bol Llanllyfrydog Llanallgo

Mount Llanfwrog Llanerchymedd Llanfihangel Tref-Beirdd

Stack A 5025 B 5110 Benllech

Kingsland Llanfachraeth Coedana Red Wharf

HOLY A 5 A N G L E S E Y B 5112 Capel Coch Bay Penmon Priory

ISLAND Llyn Llywenan Llanbedr-goch Red Wharf Bwrdd

Tre Arddur Bay Llanynghenedl Trefor Arthur

A 5 5025 B 5109 Llangwyllog B 5110 Llanddona Llangoed

Rhoscolyn Bodedern B 5109 Tregaian Mynydd Llwydiarth

Bryngwran Llanfaes Tyn-lon Rhos-meirch B 5109 Llanfaes

Cymmeran Bay Gwalchmai Bod-ffordd Talwrn Baron Hill

Tywyn Trewan A 4080 Llangefni Beaumaris

4

Rhosneigr Cerrigceinwen A 5114 Penmynydd Llansadwrn Lavan Sands

A 4080 Llanfihangel Groeslon Elandristiolus Pentraeth A 5025

Tycroes Sta. Llanfair pwllgwyngyll Aber Carreg Fawr

Llangwyfan B 4422 R. Cefni Gaerwen A 5 Llanddaniel A 545 Cymlyn Tal-y-fan

Aberffraw B 4419 Malltraeth Marsh BANGOR Penrhyn Cas. Drum

A 4080 Bodorgan Llangaffo Port Penrhyn Moel Wnion

Hermon Malltraeth Yard Brynsiencyn A 4080 A 4087 Aber Falls

Aberffraw Bay B 4421 B 4419 Port Dinorwic Cae-llwyn Y.Drosgl Koed Fras

Malltraeth Sands R. Braint Llanidan A 487 Bethesda Dolgarro

Newborough Llangeinwen B 4419 Gerlan Branch-melyn Pont Dolgarro

Malltraeth B. Newborough A 4080 B 4366 Rhiwlas Llyn Eigiau

Llanddwyn I. Warren B 4366 Penrhyn Carnedd Llewelyn

Llanddwyn Bay A 4080 Bethel Llanddeiniolen Quarries The Saddle

5

C A E R N A R V O N CAERNARVON Llanrug Deiniolen Carnedd Dafydd

B A Y Aber Menai Llanberis Dinorwic A 5

Llanfaglan Cwm-y-glo Llyn Ogwen

Foryd Bont-newydd Llyn Padarn Capel Curig A 56

Dinas A 4085 Rhostryfan Llyn Peris Glyder-fach A 4086

Llanwnda Waen-fawr Nant Peris Y Garn Bethania

A 499 Betws Garmon Moel Glyder-fawr Llyn Llydaw Mymbyr Moel Siabod

Llandwrog Eilio A 4086

A 4085 Nant-y-gwryd Dolwyddelan

Groeslon B 4418 Snowdon Nant Gwynant A 496

Pen-y-groes Carmel Mynydd Summit A 498

Nantlle Mawr Glaslyn Llyn Gwynant

Tal-y-sarn Llyn Cwellyn Rhyd-ddu

Caen-y-morfa Nantlle-uchaf Y Garn Yr Aran Llyn Dinas

Carnedd Goch C A E R N A R V O N

Capel uchaf Llanllyfni Pant-glas A 487

6

Trefor Clynnog fawr A 4085 Moel Hebog Beddgelert Blaenau Festiniog

Yr Eifl Bwlch Mawr Pass of B 4414

The Rivals Y Gyrn-ddu Aber-Glaslyn Tan-y

Llanaelhaiarn Mynydd Brynkir Pont Aber Glaslyn Nantmor Moelwyn A 4108

Cefn Cennin Garn Dolbenmaen Moel Ddu Moelwyn Bach Bethania

Llithfaen B 4417 Cefn-caer-ferch Dolbenmaen A 496 Ffestiniog B 4391

Llyn Glasfryn Ynys Ddu B 4411 A 4085 B 4410 A 4407

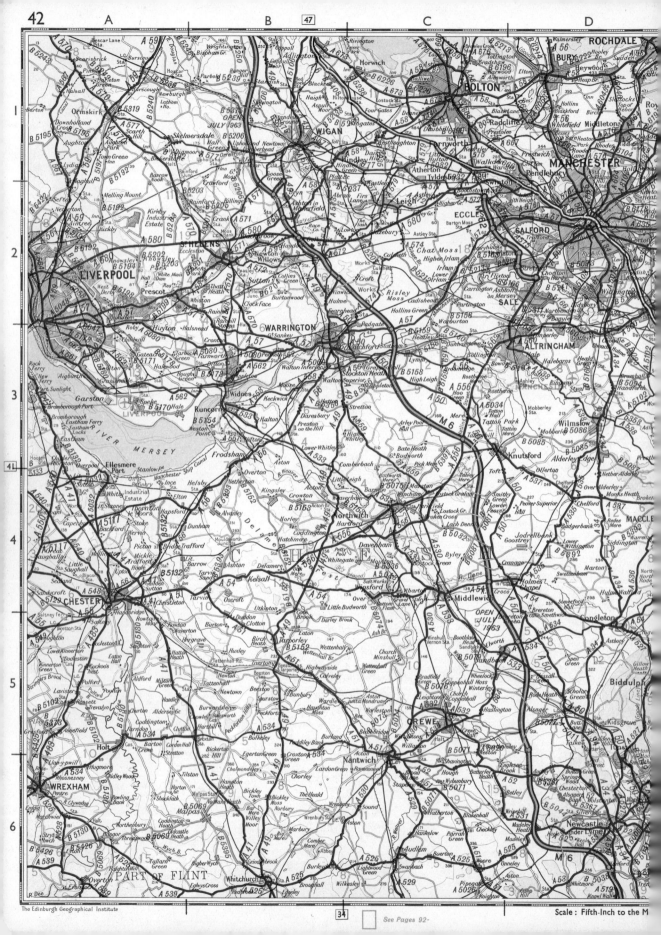

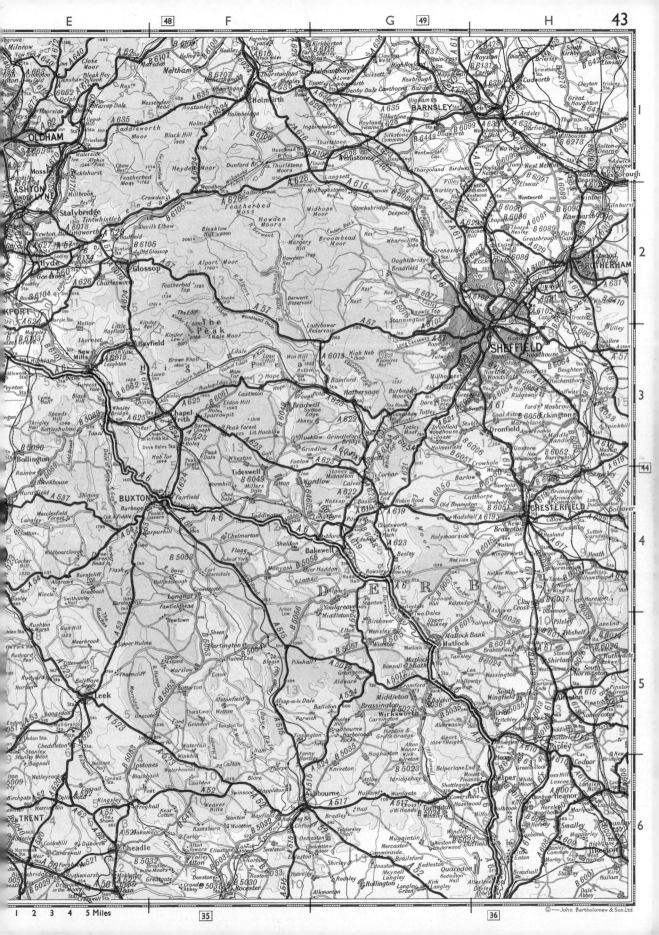

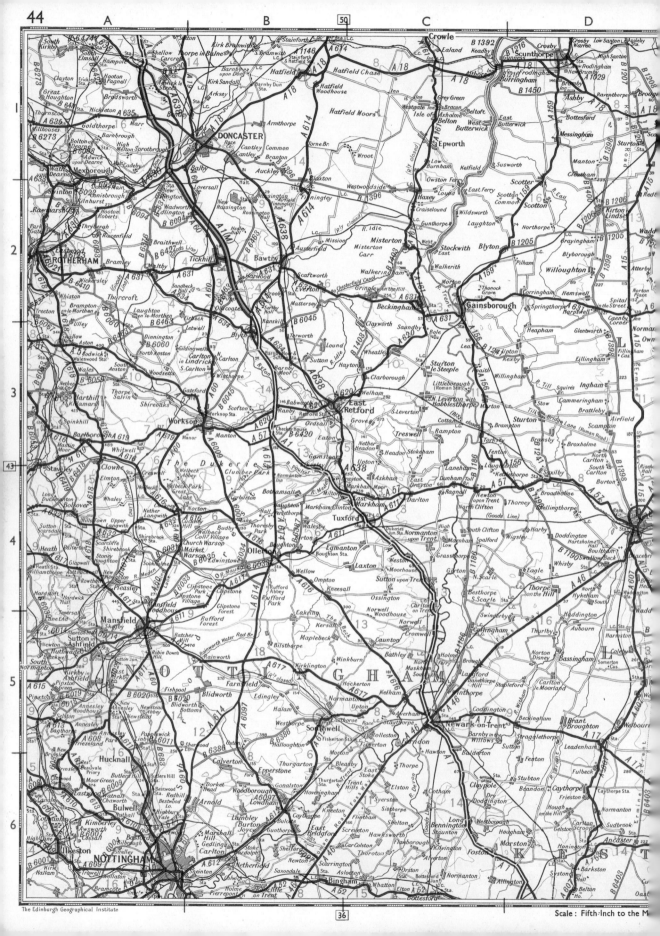

Scale: Fifth-Inch to the M

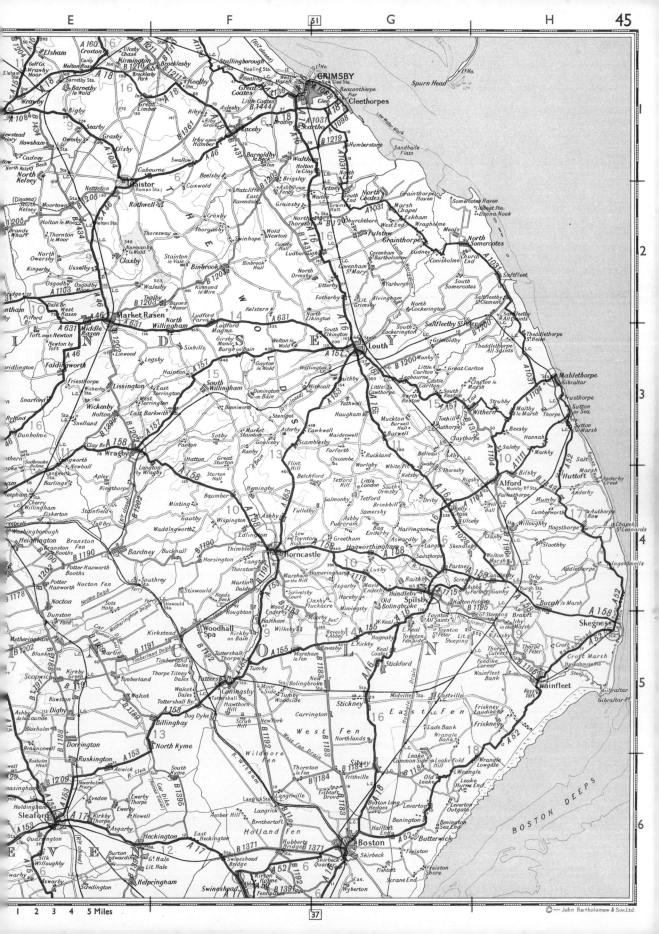

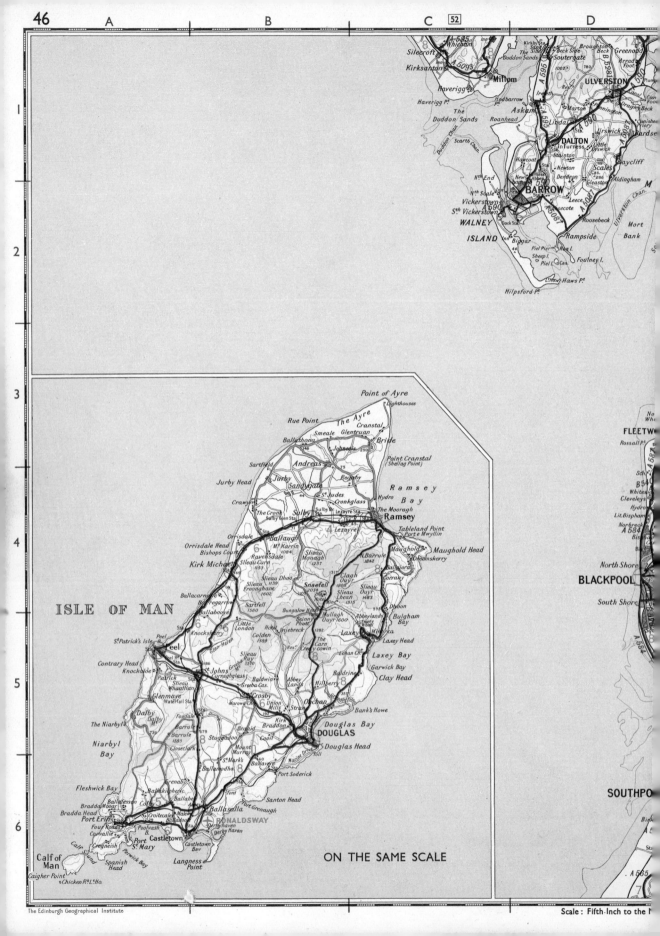

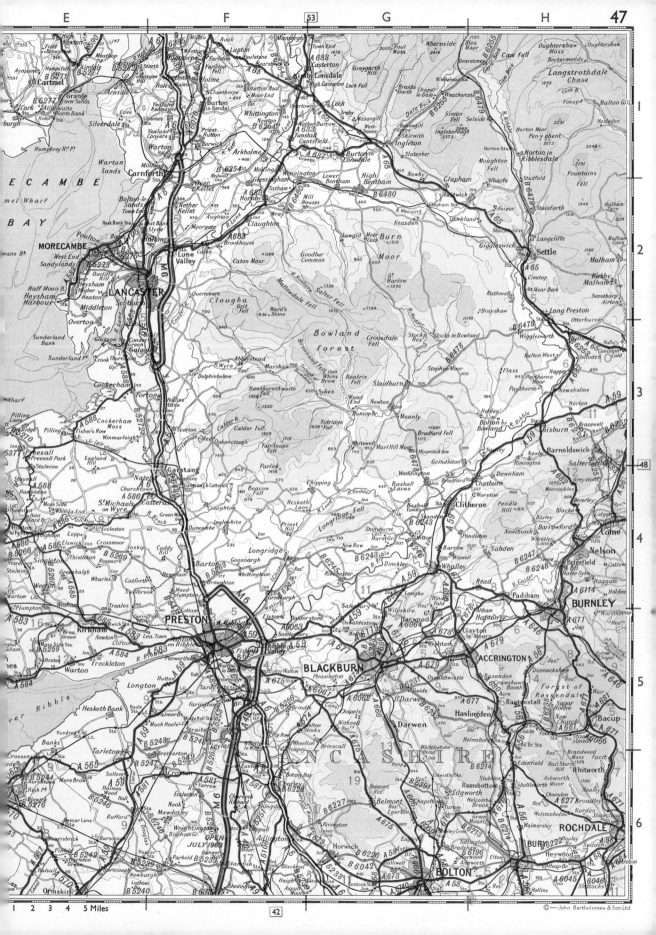

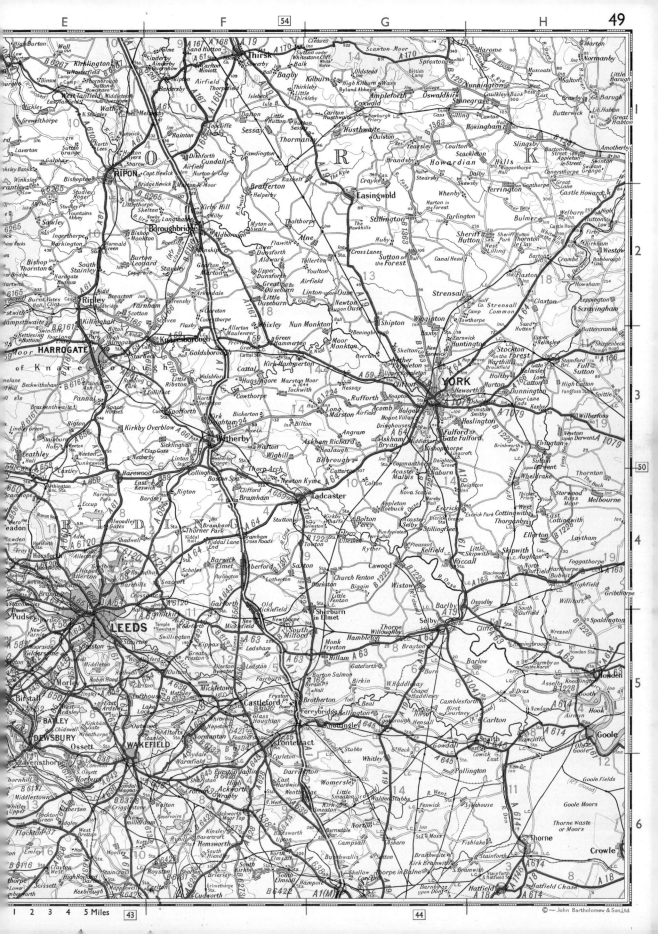

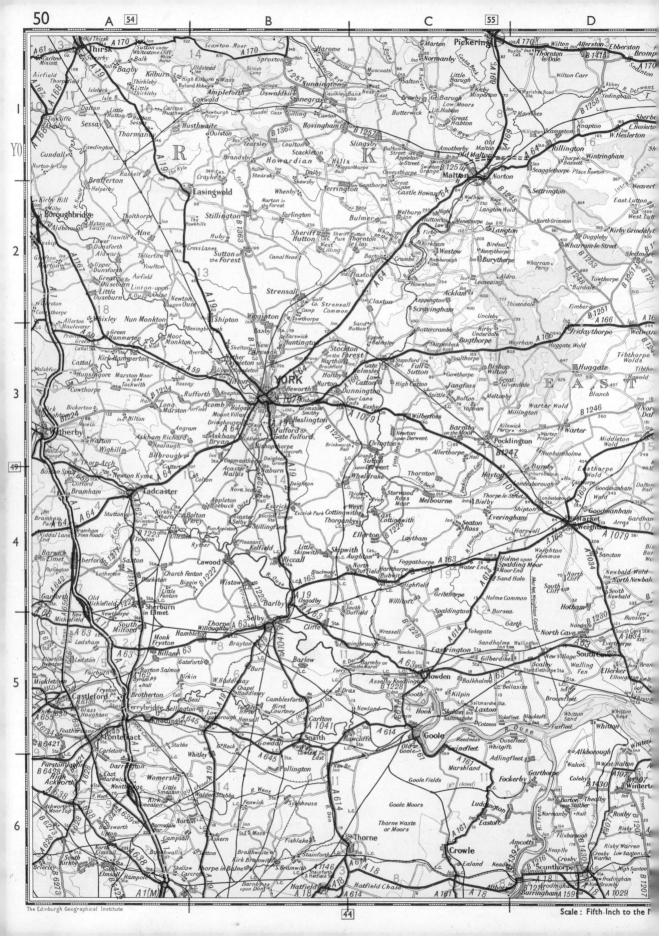

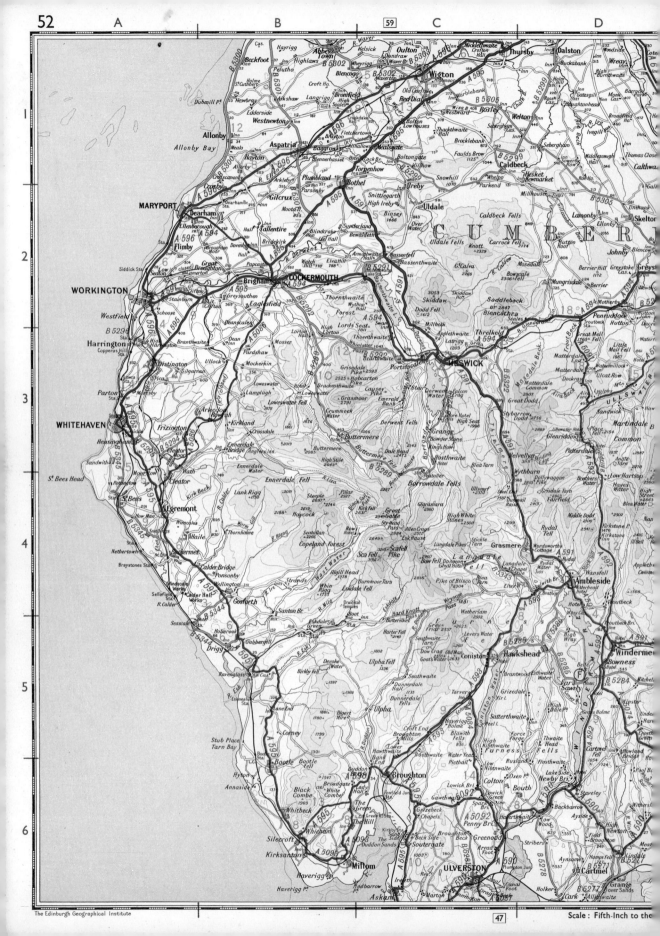

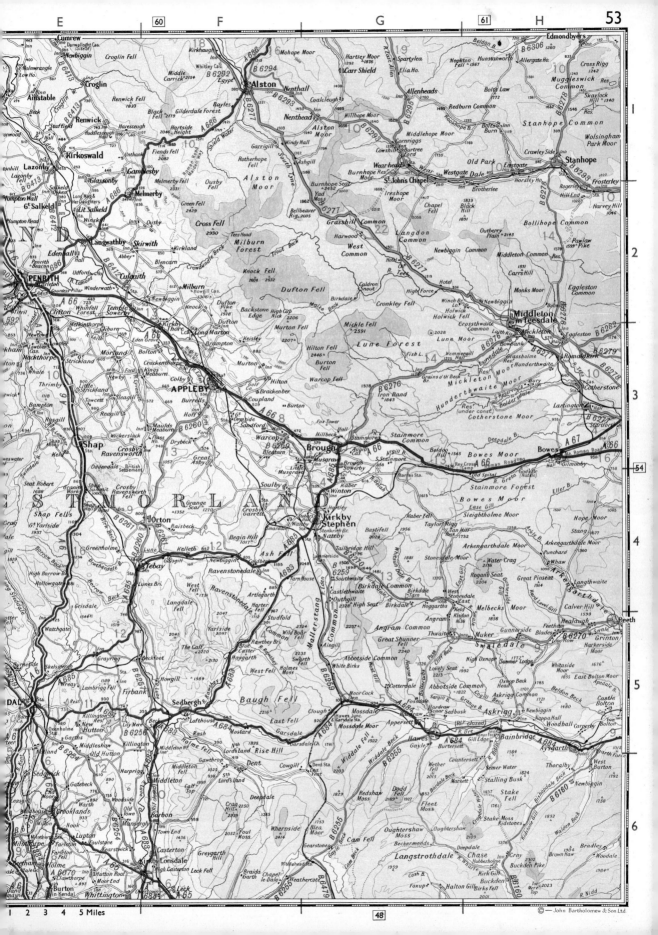

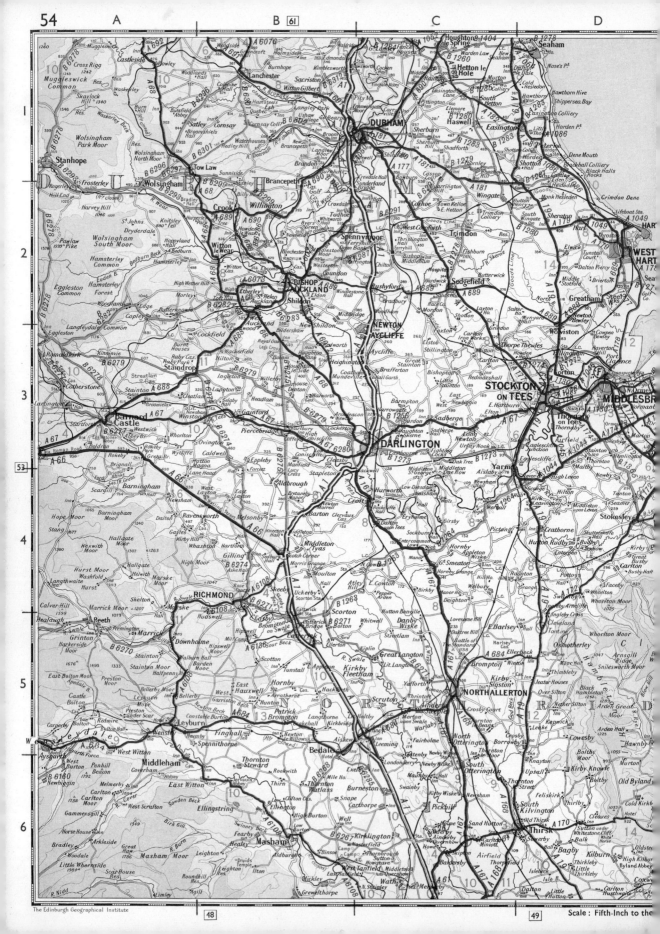

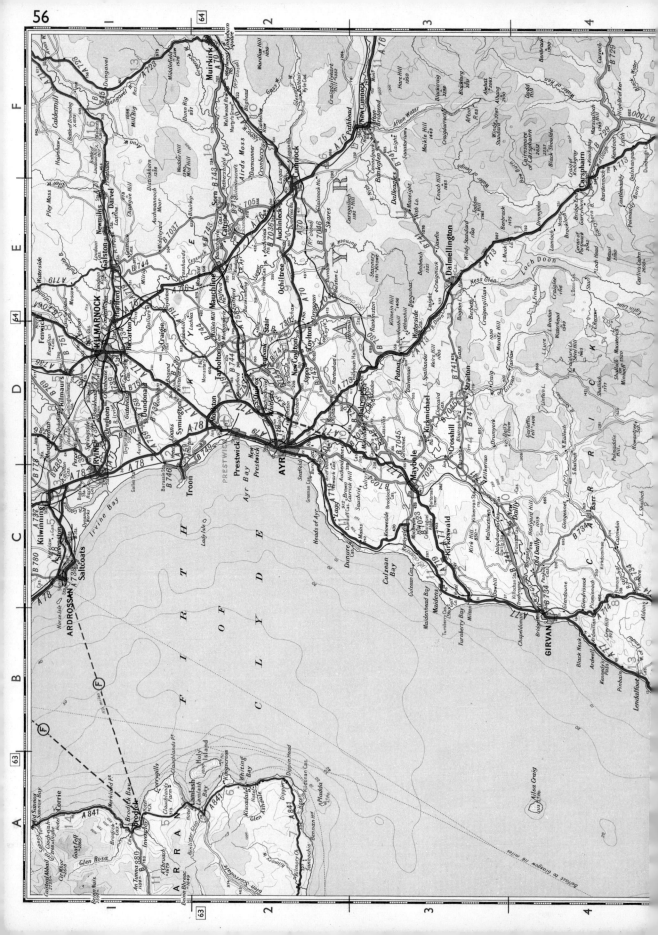

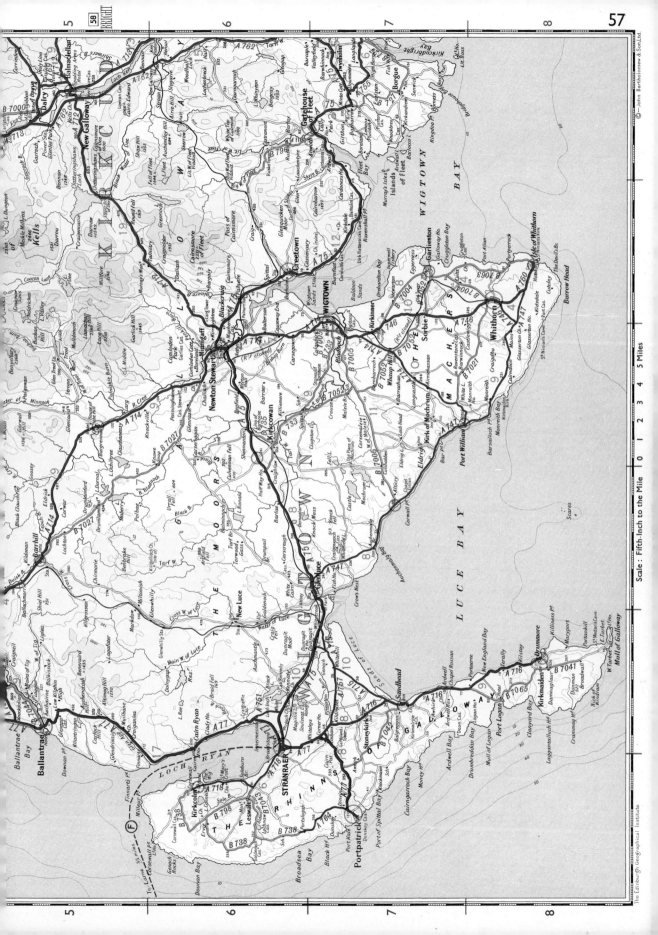

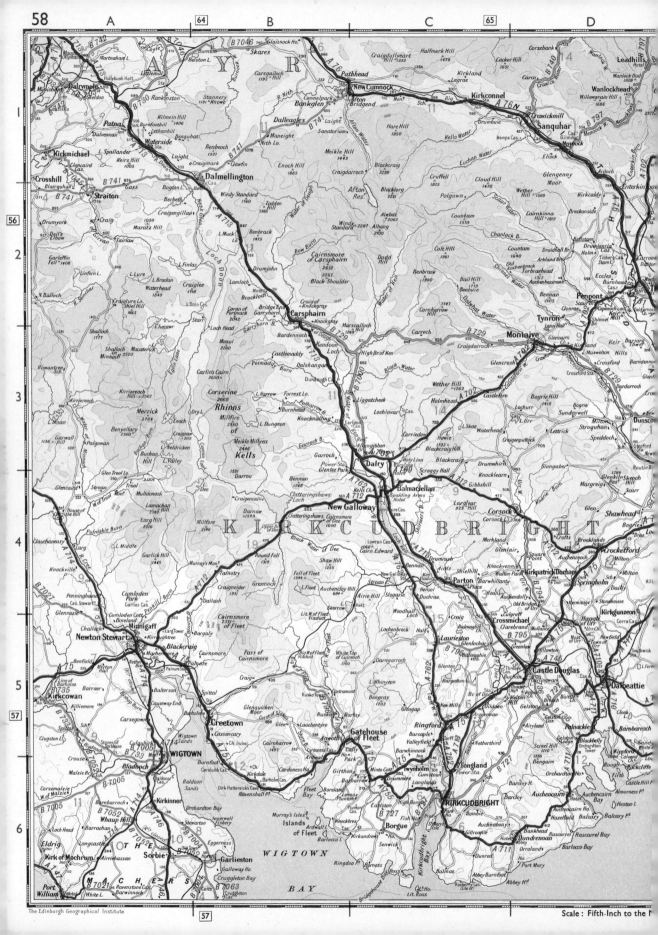

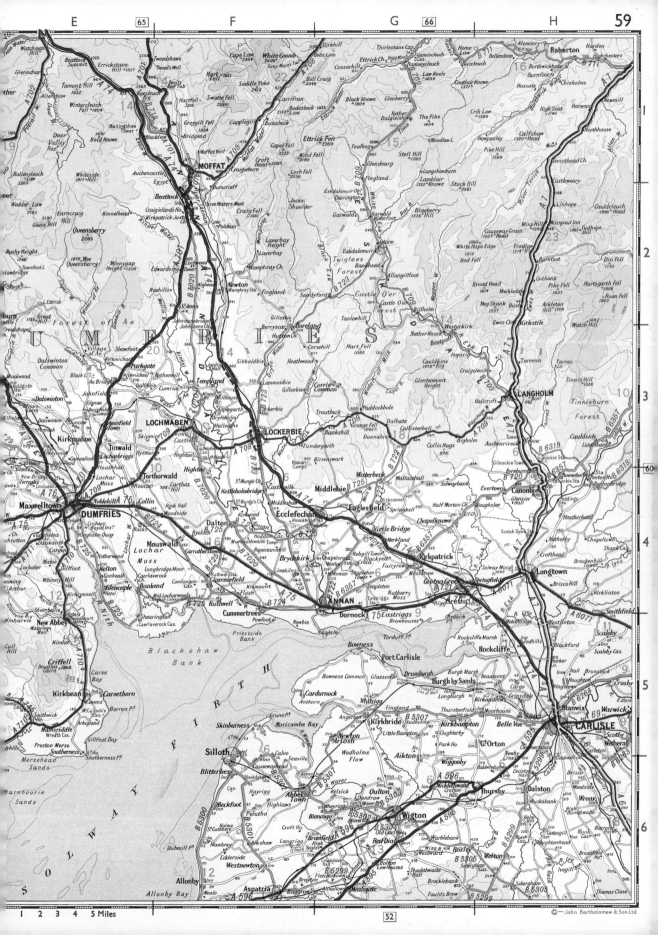

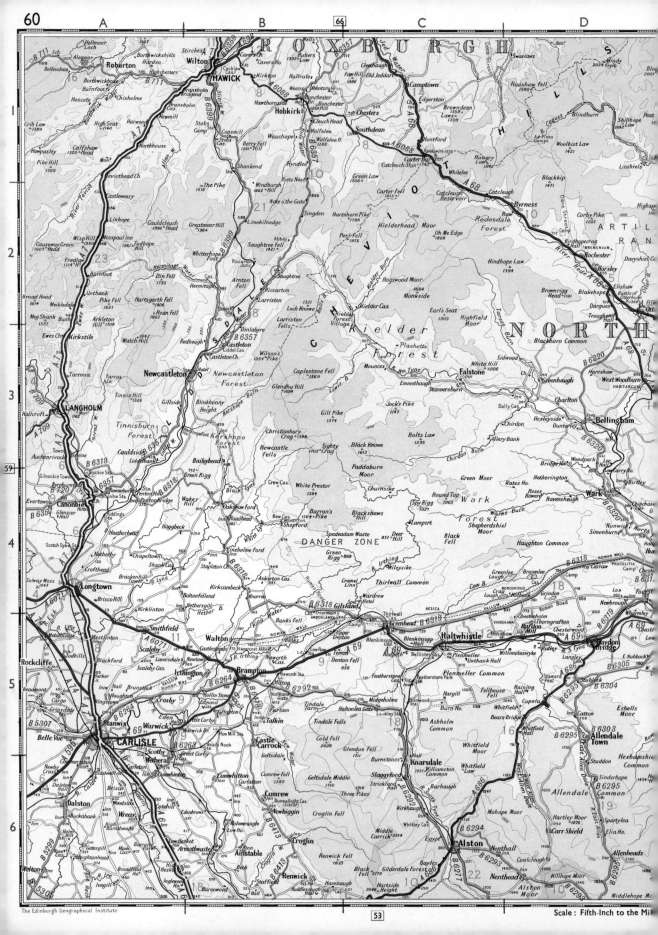

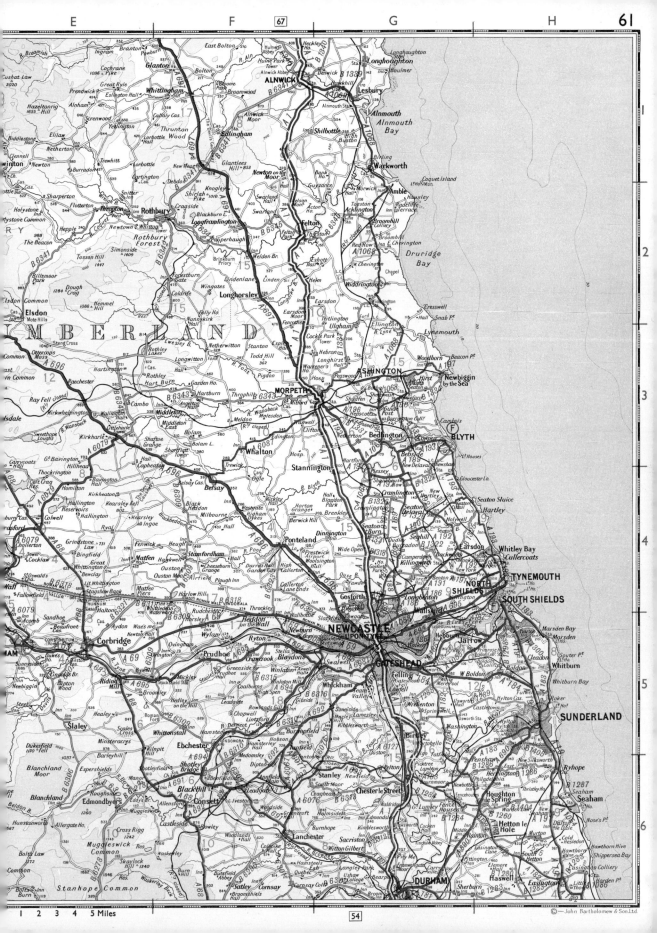

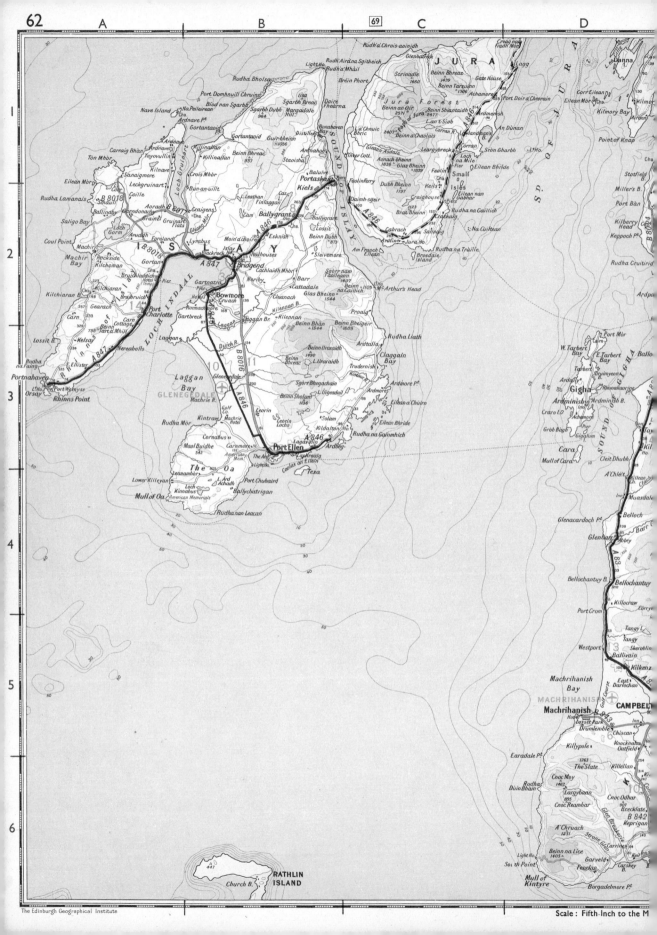

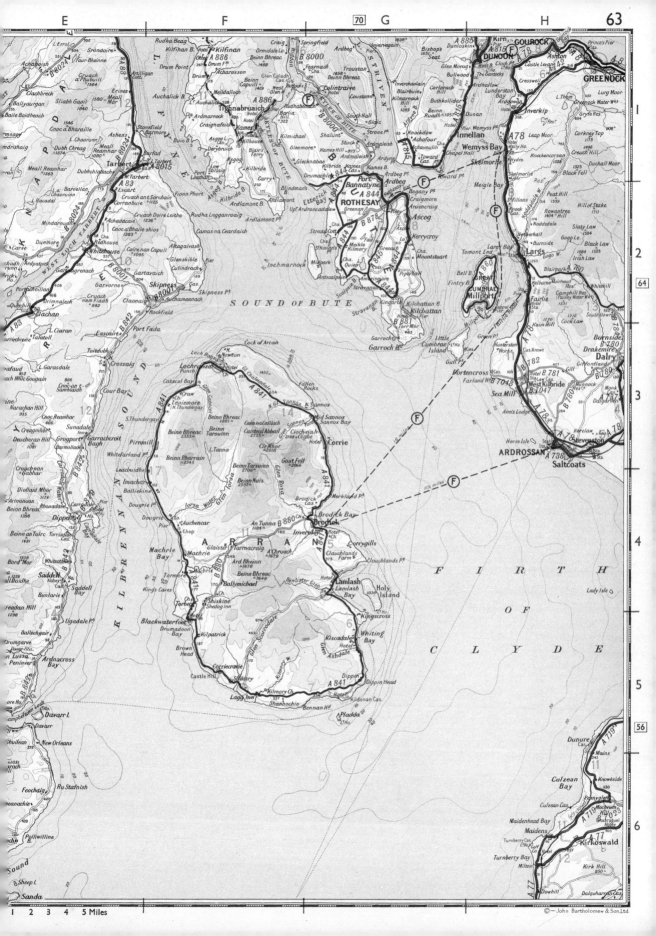

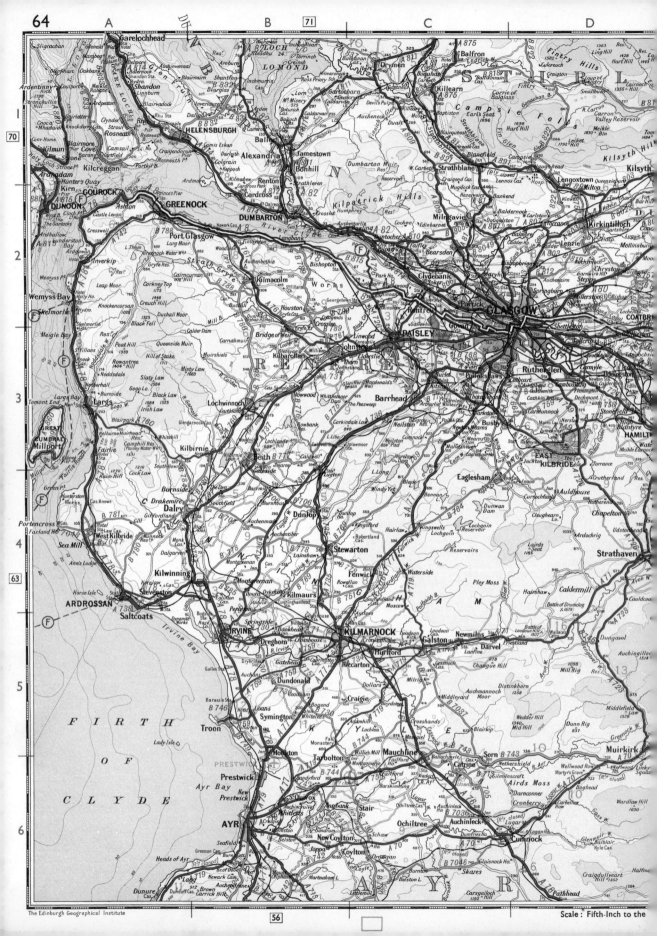

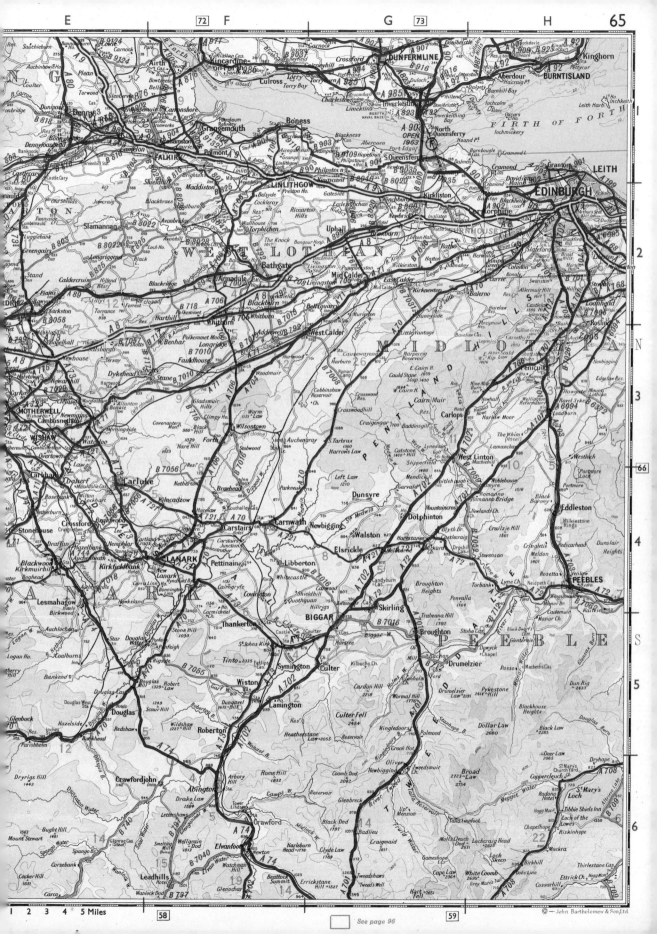

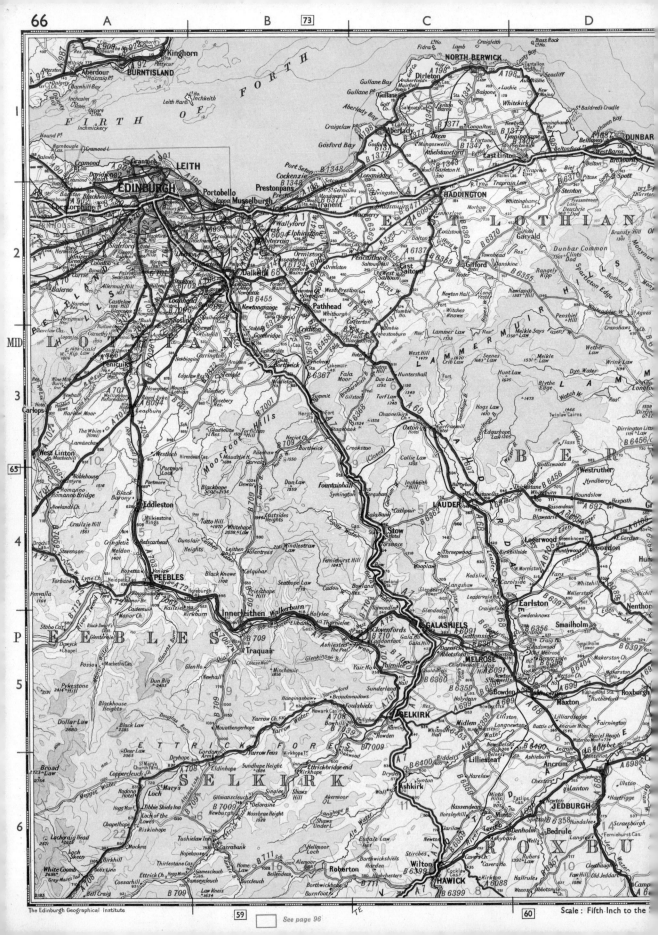

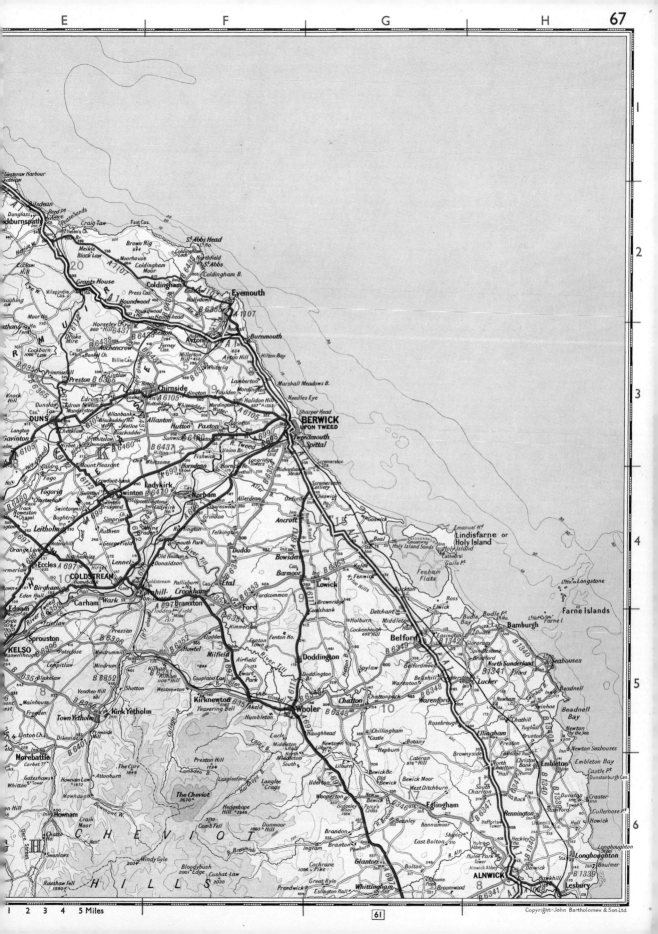

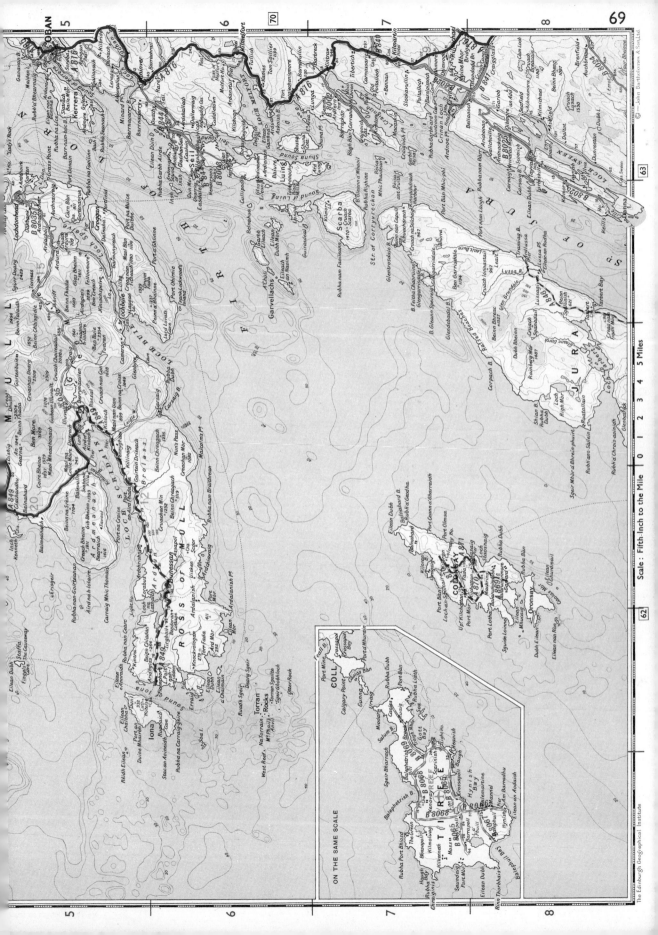

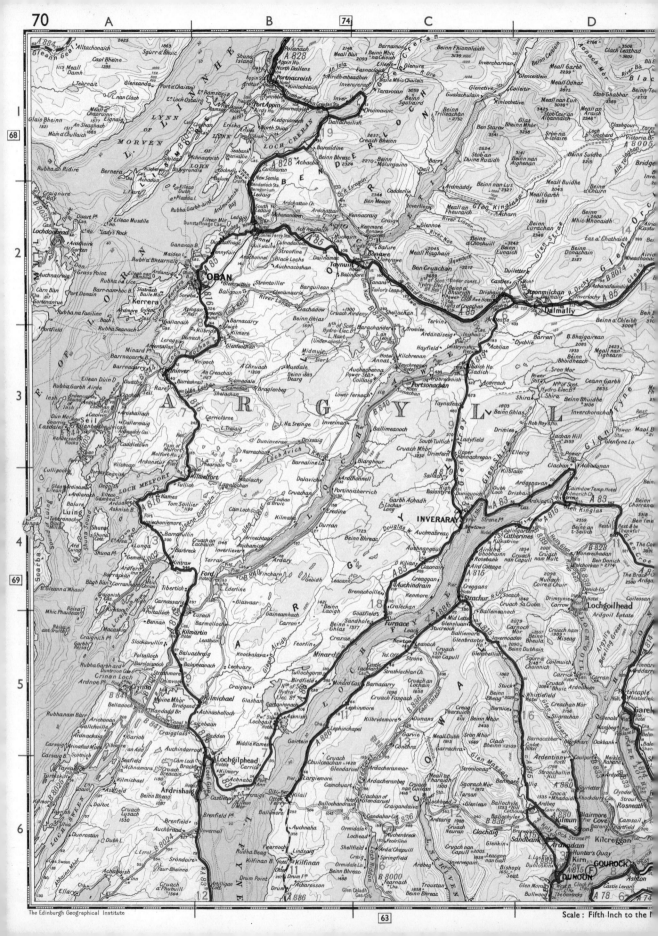

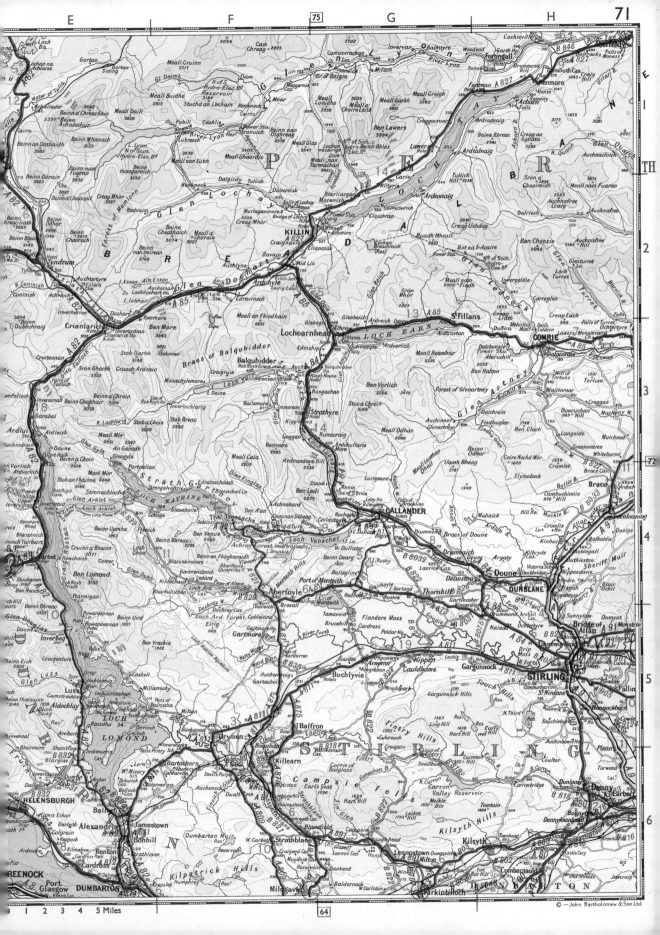

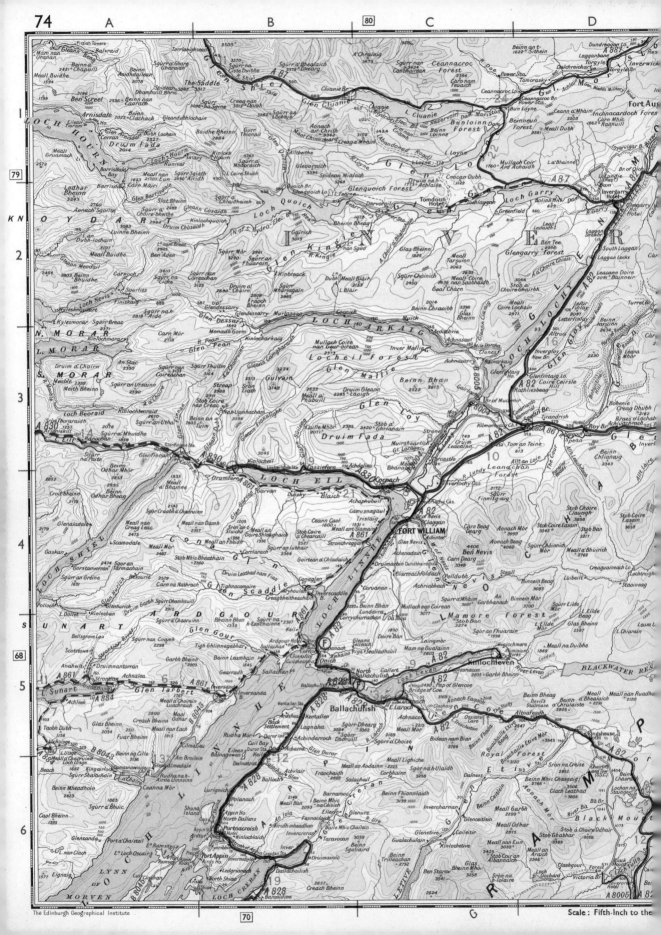

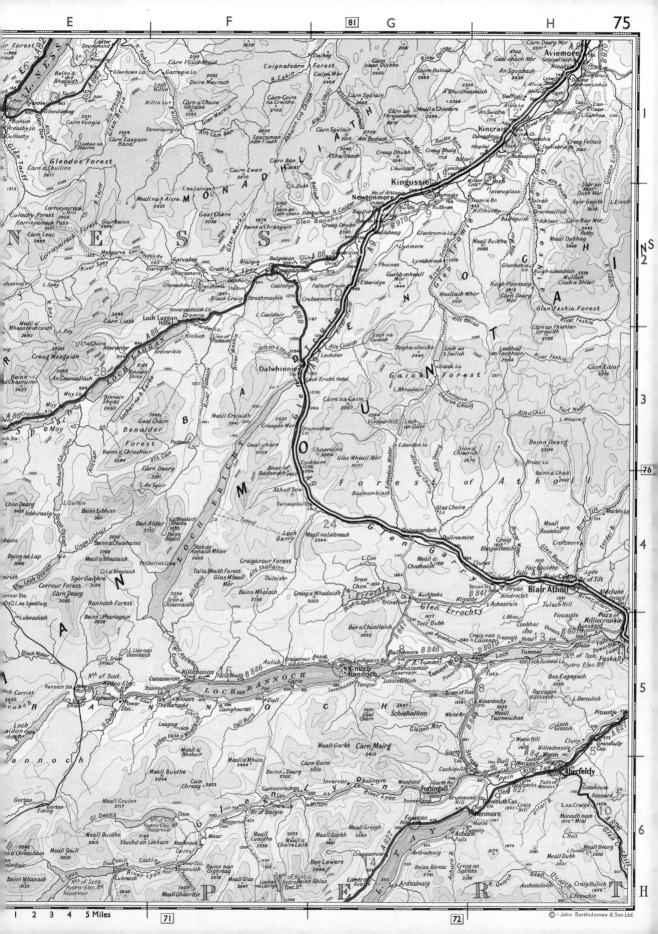

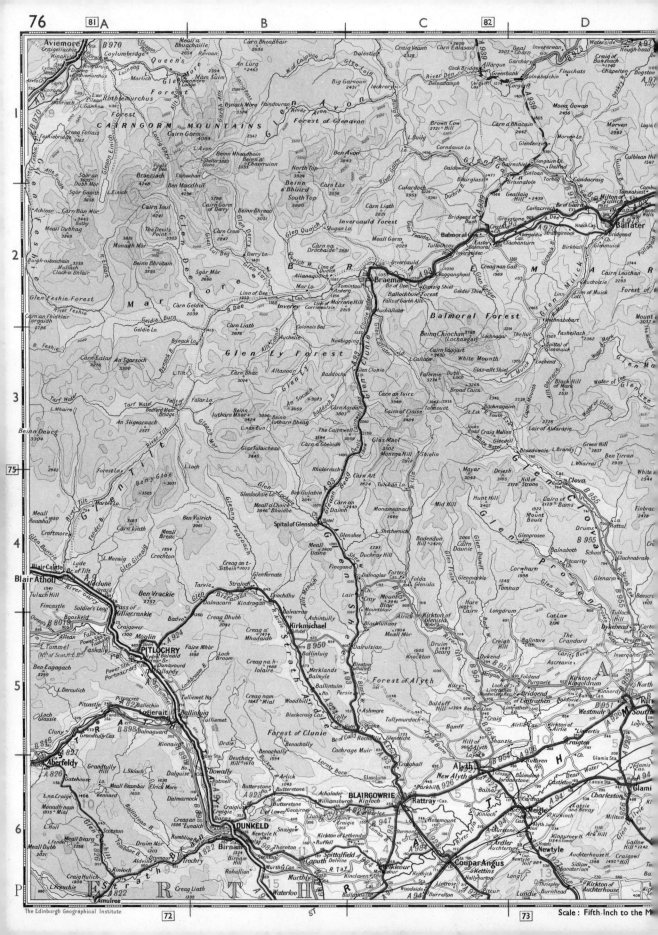

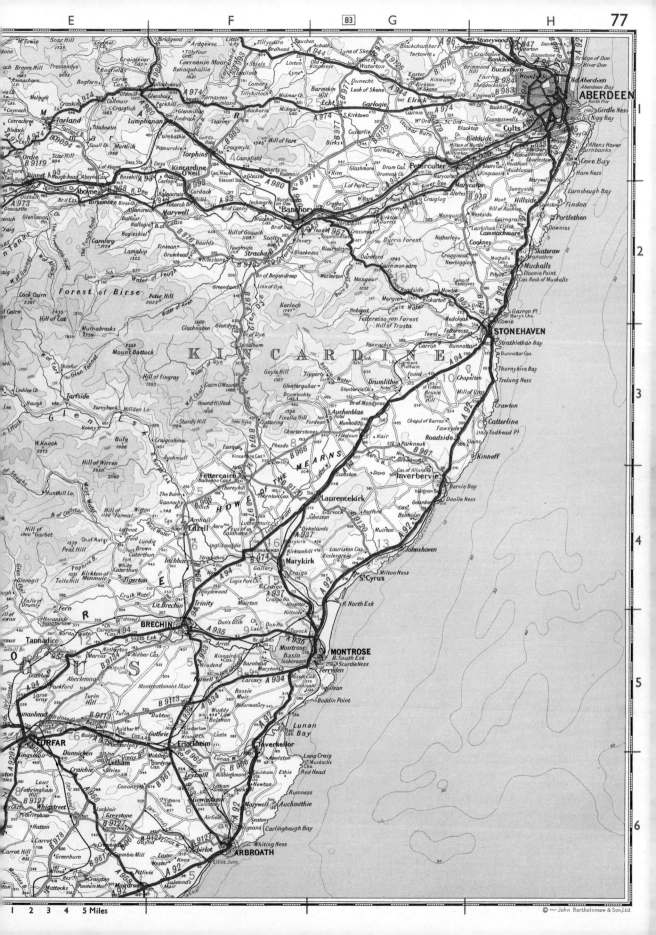

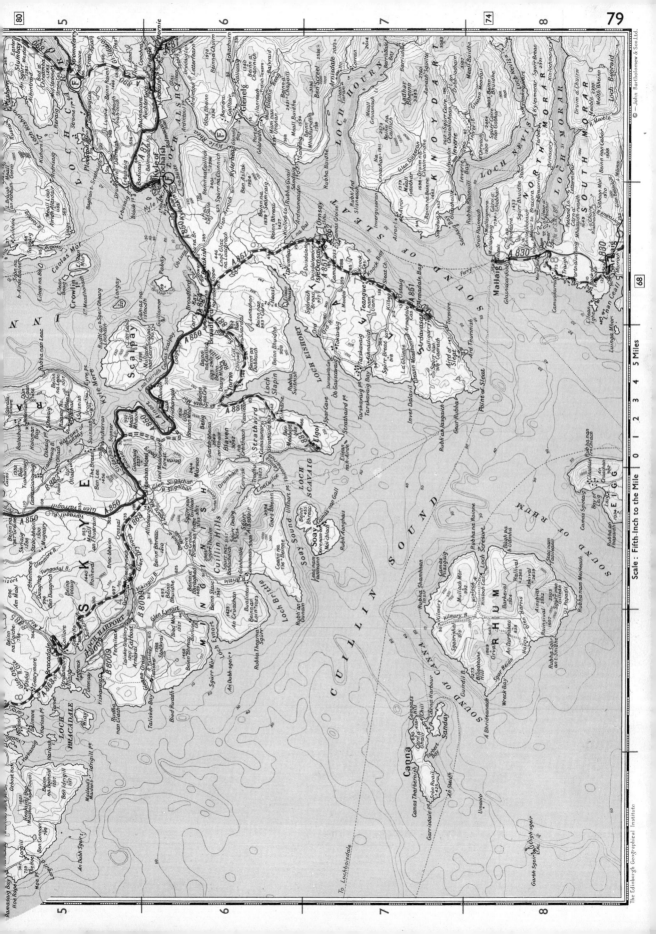

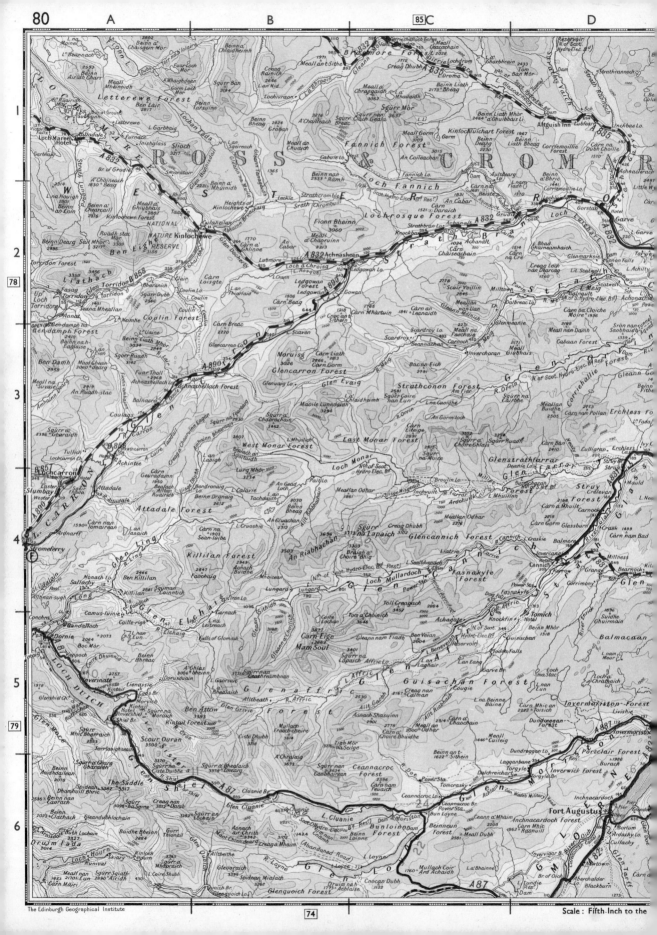

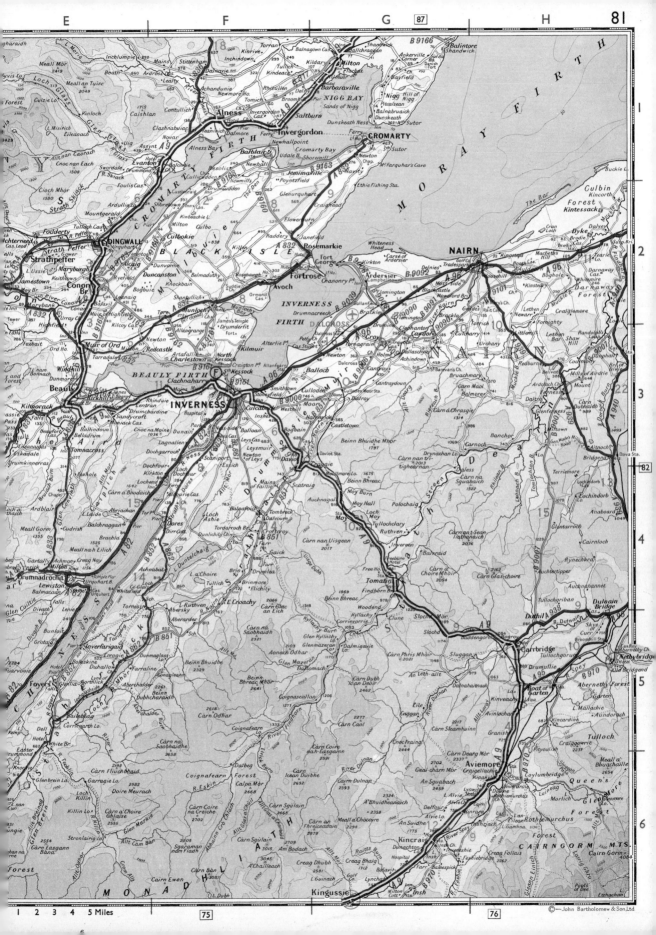

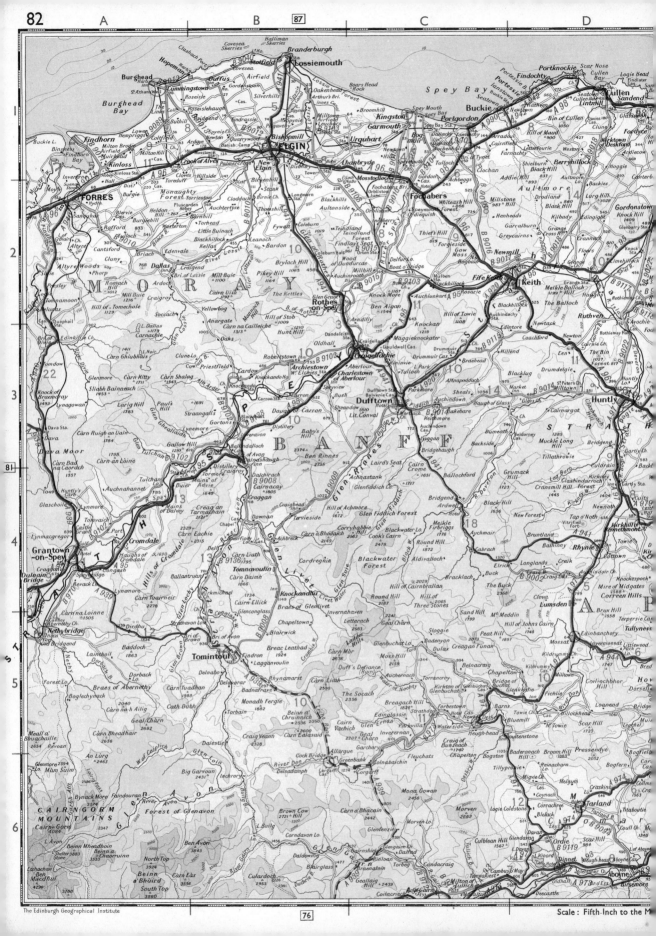

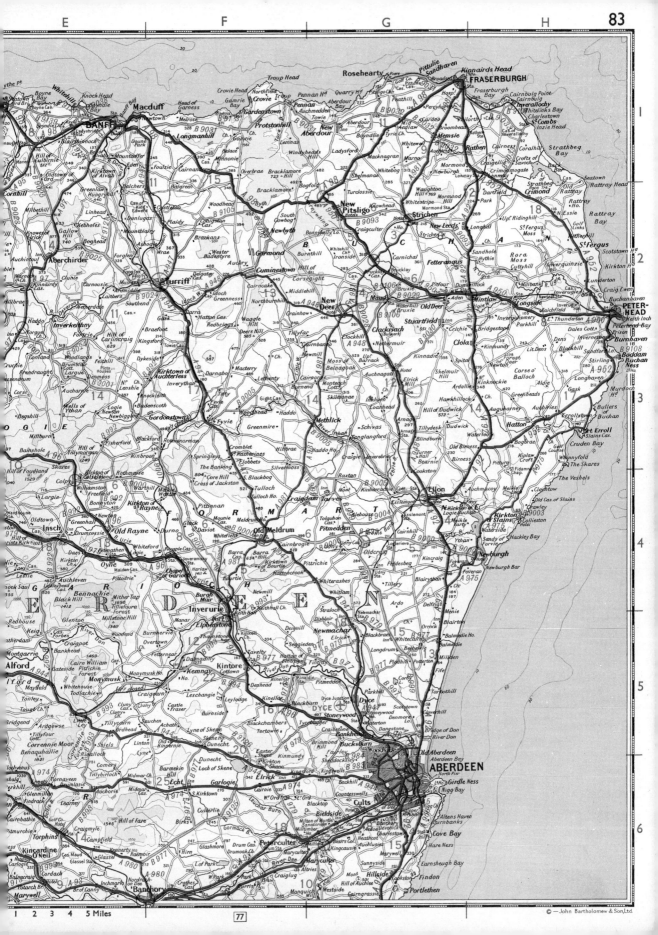

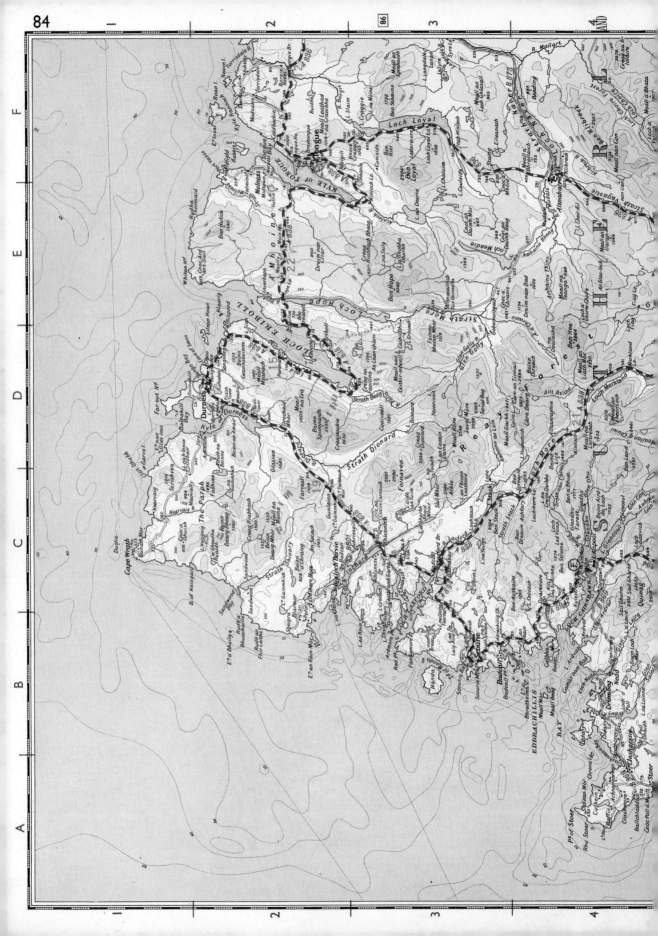

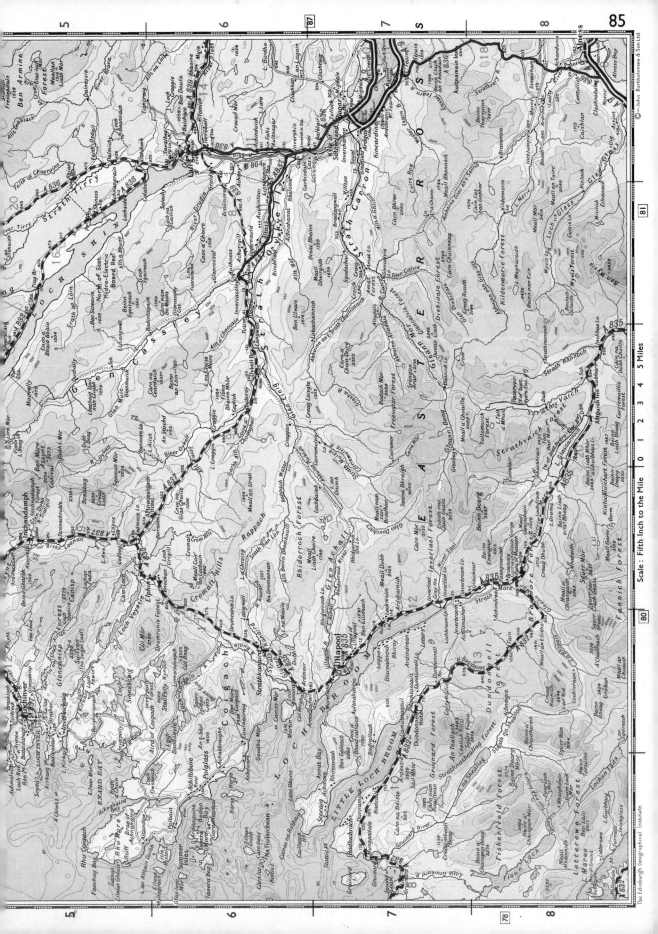

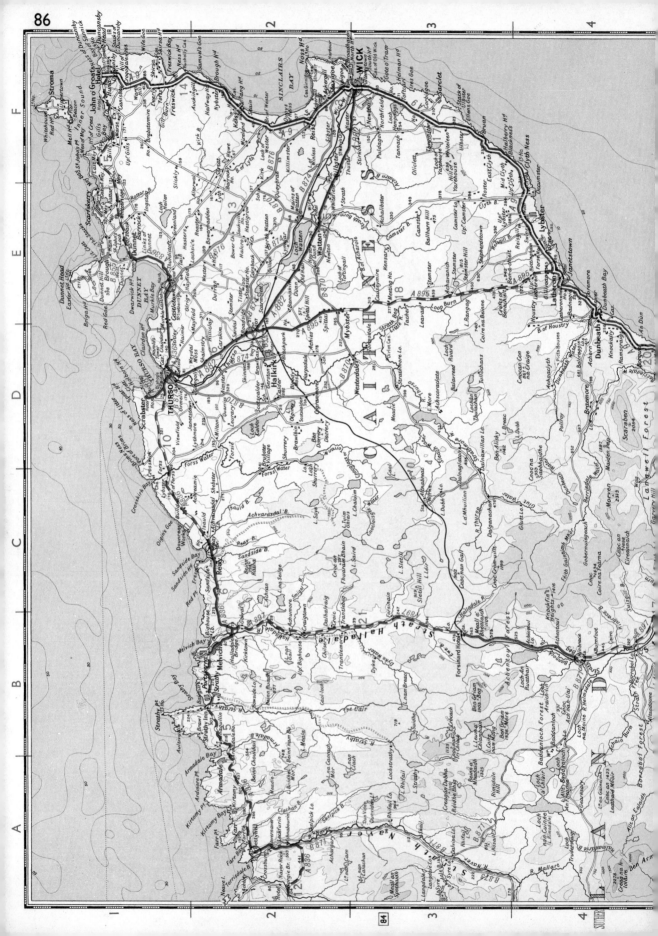

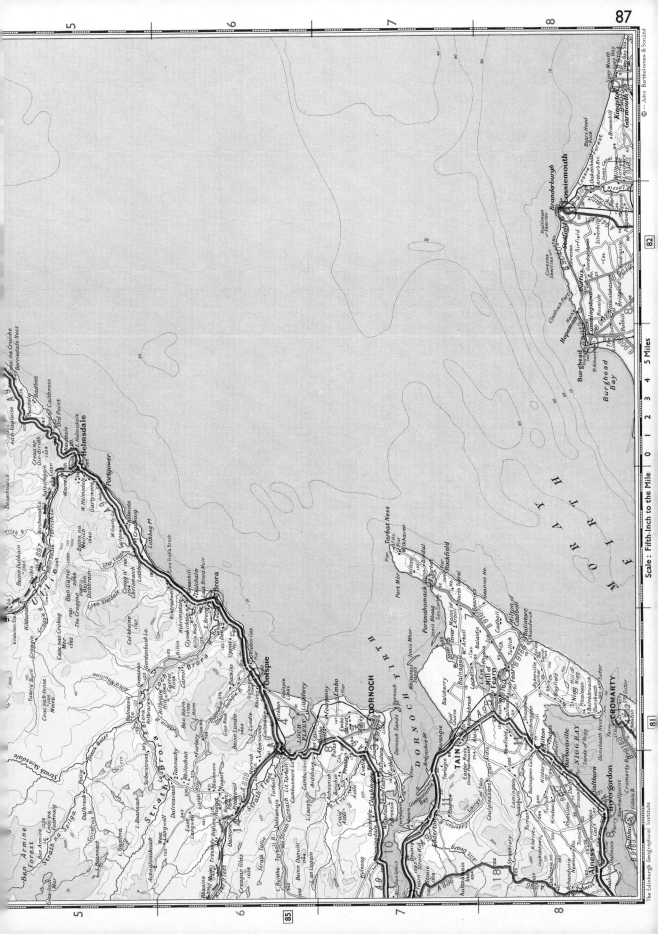

Scale : Fifth-Inch to the Mile

| 1 | 0 | 1 | 2 | 3 | 4 | 5 Miles |

82

81

85

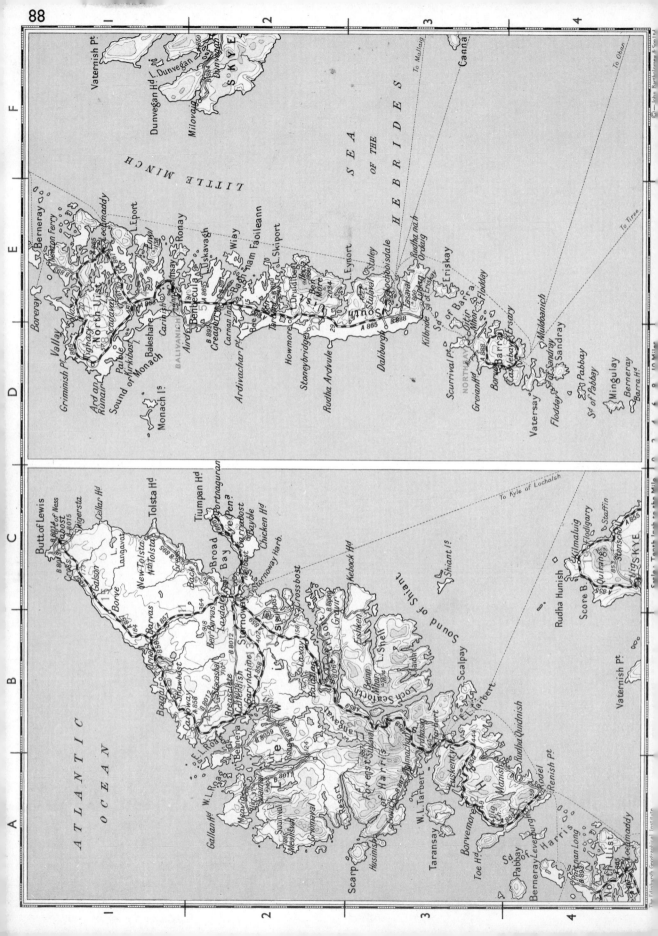

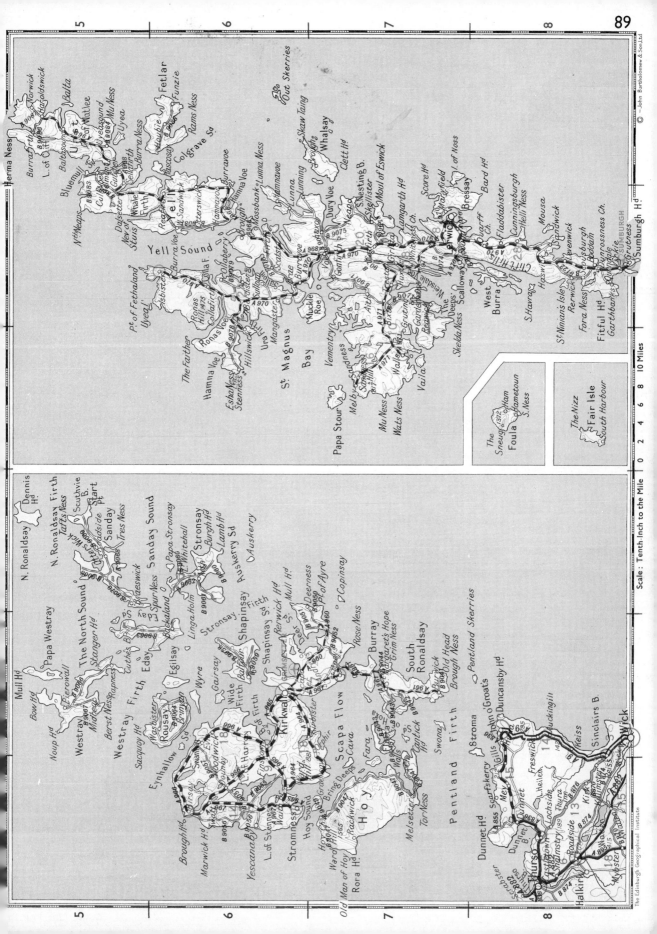

Oxford

A40

Basingstoke

KINGSBURY GREEN

GOLDERS GREEN

Highgate Golf Course

PRESTON

Barn Hill

A 500

A 406

Hampstead Golf Course

HI

Brent Reservoir

Hendon

North Circular

Road

Way

CHILD'S HILL

NORTH END

Hampstead

Highgate Ponds

Heath

NEASDEN

Edgware Road

Finchley Road

HAMPSTEAD

Hampstead Ponds

WEMBLEY

Wembley Stadium

CRICKLEWOOD

Fever Hosp.

Hosp.

BRONDESBURY

Primrose Hill

WILLESDEN

Hosp.

KILBURN

ALPERTON

North Circular Road

Grand Union Canal

HARLESDEN

ST JOHN'S WOOD

Zoological Gardens

Twyford Abbey

Cen. Middlesex Hospital

KENSAL GREEN

Maida Vale

Lord's Cricket Ground

Regen Pe

PARK ROYAL

Willesden Junction

Western

PADDINGTON

Sta

A 40

Harlesden Lane

Wormwood Scrubs

Infirmary

Hosp.

Paddington Station

Hosp.

Edgware Road

Marylebone Rd

R. Brent

Avenue

Prison

Hospital

Westway

White City Stadium

NOTTING HILL

BAYSWATER

Bayswater

Marble Arch

Hyde Park

ACTON

EAST ACTON

QPR Football Ground

SHEPHERDS BUSH

Holland Park Ave.

Kensington

Gardens

Hyde Corr

EALING

Holland Road

KENSINGTON

Palace

The Serpentine

SOUTH ACTON

Gunnersbury Avenue

BEDFORD PARK

Goldhawk Road

Holland Park

Kensington

Road

Royal Albert Hall

Science Museums

Gunnersbury Park

A 406

Olympia

BROMPTON

GUNNERSBURY

Chiswick

High

Road

HAMMERSMITH

EARLS COURT

Fulham Road

CHELSEA

Great West

Gunnersbury Rd

Earls Court Exhibition

Hosp.

Brentford Football Gd.

Kew Br

CHISWICK

Fever Hosp.

Batter Park

Palace

CASTELNAU

Chelsea Football Gd.

KEW

Mortlake Road

Reservoirs (M.W.B.)

RIVER

FULHAM

WALHAM GREEN

BATTERSEA

Royal Botanic Gardens

A 205

Barn Elms Pk.

Fulham Football Ground

PARSONS GREEN

Power Sta

NORTH SHEEN

Fulham Palace

Putney Bridge

Clapham Junc.

Royal Mid-Surrey Golf Course

BARNES

Barnes Common

THAMES

A 316

MORTLAKE

Upper

Richmond

Road

PUTNEY

Battersea Rise

EAST SHEEN

Beverley Brook

Roehampton Golf Course

Putney Hill

Wandsworth High St.

A 219

A 3

RICHMOND

WANDSWORTH

1 Mile

©—John Bartholomew & Son, Ltd.

LIVERPOOL

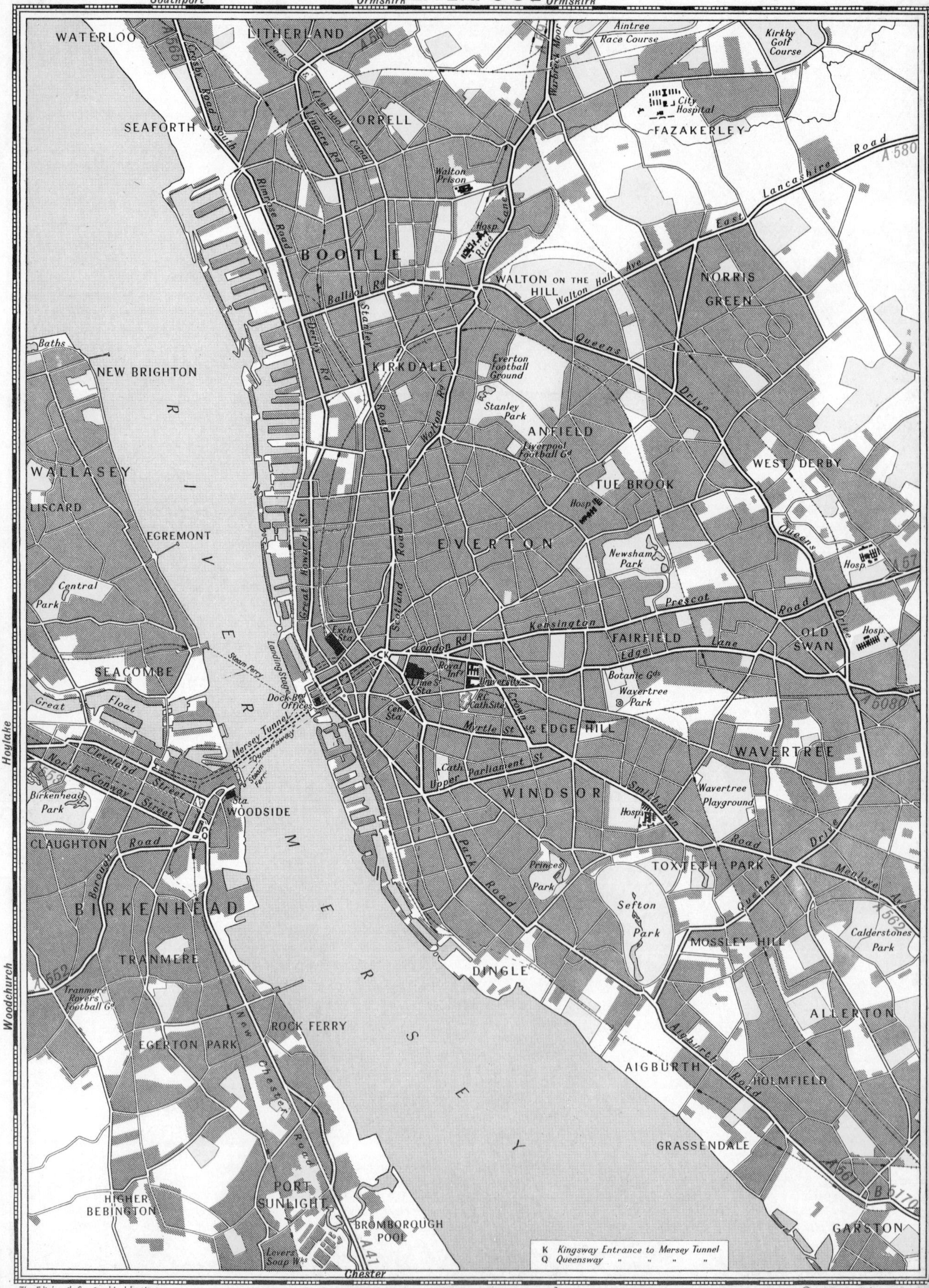

Southport Ormskirk *Ormskirk*

WATERLOO

LITHERLAND

SEAFORTH

ORRELL

Aintree Race Course

Kirkby Golf Course

City Hospital

FAZAKERLEY

Walton Prison

BOOTLE

Hosp

WALTON ON THE HILL

NORRIS GREEN

KIRKDALE

Walton Hall Ave

Queens Drive

NEW BRIGHTON

Baths

Everton Football Ground

Stanley Park

ANFIELD

WEST DERBY

Liverpool Football Gd

WALLASEY

LISCARD

TUE BROOK

EGREMONT

Hosp

EVERTON

Newsham Park

Hosp

Central Park

Kensington

FAIRFIELD

OLD SWAN

SEACOMBE

Great Float

Exch Sta

London Rd

Edge Lane

Royal Infr

Lime St Sta

University

Botanic Gd

Wavertree Park

Mersey Tunnel

Dock Bd Offices

Cen Sta

RC Cath Site

Steam Ferry

Myrtle St

EDGE HILL

WAVERTREE

Cleveland Street

Conway Street

Queensway

Cath Upper

Parliament St

WINDSOR

Wavertree Playground

Birkenhead Park

Sta

WOODSIDE

Hosp

Smithdown

CLAUGHTON

Princes Park

Sefton Park

TOXTETH PARK

BIRKENHEAD

Park Road

MOSSLEY HILL

Calderstones Park

TRANMERE

Tranmere Rovers Football Gd

DINGLE

ALLERTON

EGERTON PARK

ROCK FERRY

AIGBURTH

HOLMFIELD

New Chester Road

GRASSENDALE

HIGHER BEBINGTON

PORT SUNLIGHT

GARSTON

BROMBOROUGH POOL

Lovers Soap Wks

Chester

K	Kingsway Entrance to Mersey Tunnel
Q	Queensway " " "

The Edinburgh Geographical Institute

Scale : One Inch to Mile 0 ½ 1 Mile

© —John Bartholomew & Son Ltd

Bury · Rochdale

STAND
BESSES O' TH' BARN
WHITEFIELD
RHODES
MIDDLETON
MIDDLETON JUNC.
ALKRINGTON GARDEN VILLAGE
Heaton Park Reservoir
Heaton Park Golf Course
Heaton Park
HIGHER BLACKLEY
Hosp.
PRESTWICH
Hosp.
BLACKLEY
Boggart Hole Clough
NEW MOSTON
Broadhurst Park
Failsworth Golf Course
HILTON PARK
CRUMPSALL
Hosp.
Inst.
MOSTON
BROUGHTON PARK
Old Manchester Golf Course
HARPURHEY
Hosp.
LOWER KERSAL
Race Course
CHEETHAM HILL
Queens Park
NEWTON HEATH
River Irwell
CHARLESTOWN
CHEETWOOD
COLLYHURST
Rochdale Canal
CLAYTON BRIDGE
LOWER BROUGHTON
Strangeways Prison
MILES PLATTING
Philips Park
Manchester Bolton & Bury Canal
Peel Park
Victoria Sta.
ANCOATS
CLAYTON
SEEDLEY
Exch. Sta.
BRADFORD
Chapel St.
Manchester & Ashton Canal
SALFORD
Town Hall
London Rd Sta.
Ashton Old Road
Central Sta.
HARDWICK
ORDSALL
Docks
HULME
GORTON
Manchester Ship Canal
Belle Vue Gardens
Man. Utd. Football Gd.
Victoria University
Royal Infirmary
Trafford Park
OLD TRAFFORD
LONGSIGHT
Lancs County Cricket Gd.
MOSS SIDE
RUSHOLME
STRETFORD
WHALLEY RANGE
Alexandra Park
Man City Football Gd.
Birchfields Park
LEVENSHULME
Longford Park
Platt Fields Park
Manchester Grammar Sch.
Houldsworth Golf Course
FALLOWFIELD
CHORLTON CUM HARDY
Cringle Fields Park
HEATON CHAPEL
River Mersey
CHORLTONVILLE
WITHINGTON
BURNAGE
SALE
Chorlton Golf Course
Hosp.
Golf Course
HEATON MOOR
Bridgewater Canal
WEST DIDSBURY
Fog Lane Park
Cheadle · Stockport

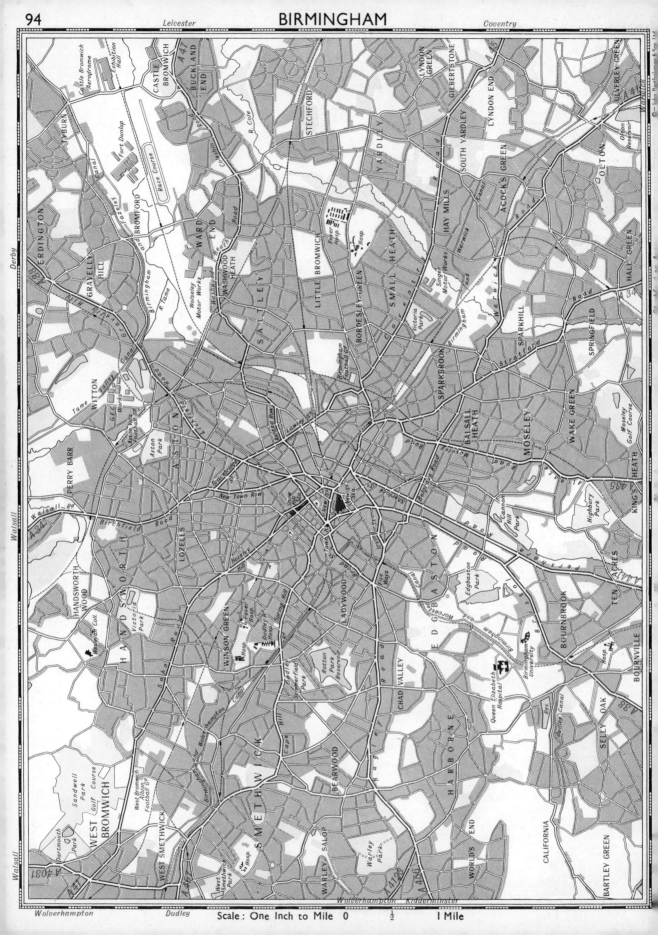

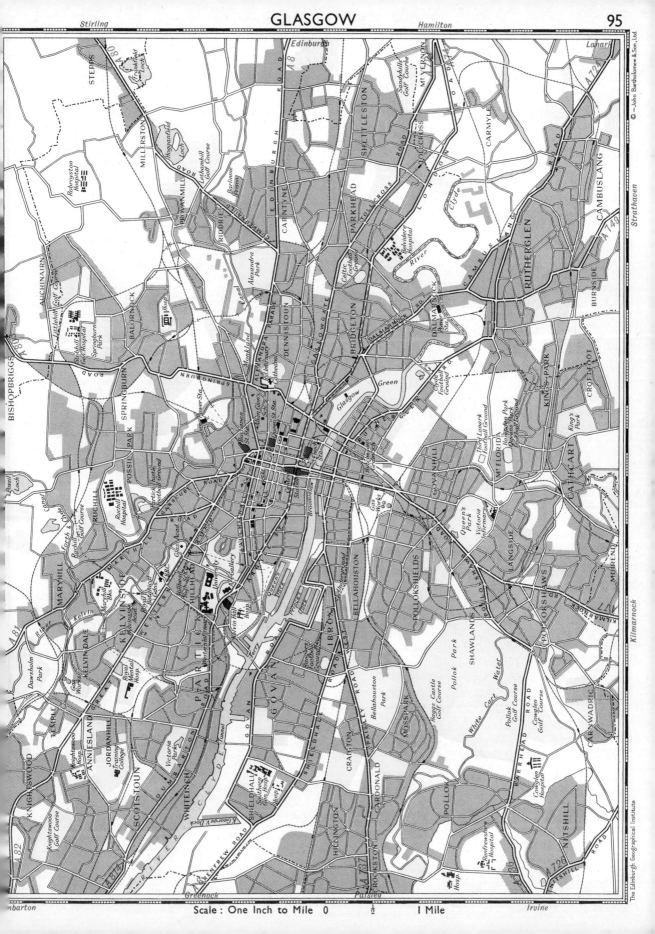

Scale: One Inch to Mile   0   ½   1 Mile

The Edinburgh Geographical Institute

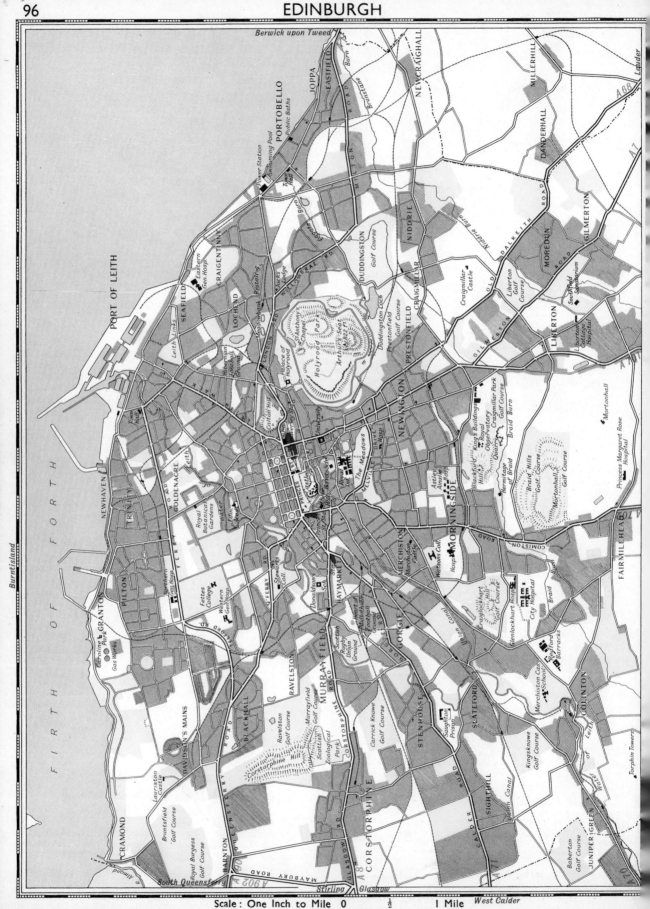

Scale : One Inch to Mile 0   ½   1 Mile

INDEX

List of Counties and Abbreviations

A'deen	Aberdeen	—	Derby	Lancs	Lancashire	Renf	Renfrew
Angl	Anglesey	—	Devon	Leics	Leicester	Ross	Ross and Cromarty
—	Angus	—	Dorset	Lincs	Lincoln	Rox	Roxburgh
—	Argyll	Dumf	Dumfries	—	London	Rutl	Rutland
—	Ayr	Dunb	Dunbarton	Mer	Merioneth	Selk	Selkirk
—	Banff	—	Durham	Middx	Middlesex	Shet	Shetland
Beds	Bedford	E. Loth	East Lothian	M'loth	Midlothian	Shrops	Shropshire (Salop)
Berks	Berkshire	—	Essex	Mon	Monmouth	Som	Somerset
—	Berwick	—	Fife	Mont	Montgomery	Staffs	Stafford
—	Bute	—	Flint	—	Moray	Stirl	Stirling
Brecon	Brecknock	Glam	Glamorgan	—	Nairn	Suff	Suffolk
Bucks	Buckingham	Glos	Gloucester	Norf	Norfolk	—	Surrey
—	Bute	Hants	Hampshire	Northants	Northampton	—	Sussex
Caern	Caernarvon	Herefs	Hereford	N'land	Northumberland	Suth	Sutherland
Caith	Caithness	Herts	Hertford	Notts	Nottingham	Warks	Warwick
Cambs	Cambridge	Hunts	Huntingdon	—	Orkney	W. Loth	West Lothian
Card	Cardigan	I'ness	Inverness	Oxon	Oxford	W'land	Westmorland
Carm	Carmarthen	—	Kent	Peebl	Peebles	Wig	Wigtown
Ches	Cheshire	Kinc	Kincardine	Pemb	Pembroke	Wilts	Wiltshire
Clack	Clackmannan	—	Kinross	—	Perth	Worcs	Worcester
Corn	Cornwall	Kirkcud	Kirkcudbright	Radn	Radnor	Yorks	Yorkshire
Cumb	Cumberland	—	Lanark				
Denb	Denbigh						

B.	Bay	Pen.	Peninsula
Br.	Bridge	Pt.	Point
C.	Cape	R.	River
co.	county	Res.	Reservoir
div.	division	S.	South
E.	East	St.	Saint
Hd.	Head	W.	West
I.	Island		
L.	Lake		
mt.	mountain		
N.	North		

Cleator Fordingbridge

Cleator	W'land	52 A4
Cleckheaton	Yorks	48 D5
Cleethorpes	Lincs	45 G1
Cloebury Mortimer	Shrops	26 B1
Clevedon	Som	15 H4
Cleveleys	Lancs	46 D4
Cley	Norf	39 E1
Clifford	Herefs	25 G3
Clifton	Lancs	42 D1
Clifton	Warks	36 B6
Clitheroe	Lancs	47 G4
Clophill	Beds	29 E4
Closeburn	Dumf	58 D2
Cloughton	Yorks	55 H5
Clova	Angus	76 D4
Clovelly	Devon	6 C3
Clovenfords	Selk	66 C5
Clowne	Derby	44 A3
Cluanie, Loch	Ross	80 B6
Cluanie Bridge	Ross	80 B6
Clun	Shrops	25 G1
Clun Forest	Shrops	34 A5
Clydach	Glam	14 C2
Clyde, R.	Dunb-Renf	64 B2
Clydebank	Dunb	64 C2
Coalville	Leics	36 A3
Coatbridge	Lanark	64 D2
Cock Bridge	A'deen	82 B6
Cockburnspath	Berwick	67 E2
Cockerham	Lancs	47 E3
Cockermouth	Cumb	52 B2
Coggeshall	Essex	30 C5
Colchester	Essex	31 E5
Cold Ashton	Glos	16 C4
Coldingham	Berwick	67 F2
Cold Norton	Essex	21 E2
Coldstream	Berwick	67 E4
Coleford	Glos	16 B1
Coleshill	Warks	35 G5
Colinsburgh	Fife	73 G4
Colinton	M'loth	65 H2
Colintraive	Argyll	63 G1
Coll, I.	Argyll	68 A3
Collingham	Notts	44 C5
Colmonell	Ayr	57 B5
Colne	Lancs	47 H4
Colonsay, I.	Argyll	69 C7
Coltishall	Norf	39 G3
Colwinston	Glam	15 E4
Colwyn Bay	Denb	41 E3
Colyton	Devon	5 G2
Combe Martin	Devon	6 D1
Comrie	Perth	72 B3
Congleton	Ches	42 D5
Congresbury	Som	16 A5
Coningsby	Lincs	45 F5
Conisbrough	Yorks	44 A2
Coniston	Lancs	52 C5
Connah's Quay	Flint	41 H4
Connel	Argyll	70 B2
Conon Bridge	Ross	81 E2
Consett	Durham	61 F6
Constantine	Corn	2 C5
Contin	Ross	81 E2
Conway	Caern	40 D4
Conwil Elvet	Carm	23 E3
Cookham	Berks	18 D3
Coombe Bissett	Wilts	9 H2
Corbridge	N'land	61 E5
Corby	Northants	36 D5
Corby Glen	Lincs	37 E2
Corfe Castle	Dorset	9 G6
Cornhill	N'land	67 F4
Cornwall, co.		3 E2
Cornwood	Devon	4 C4
Corpach	I'ness	74 C4
Corrie	Arran	63 G3
Corsham	Wilts	16 D4
Corstorphine	M'loth	65 H2
Corwen	Mer	33 H1
Coryton	Essex	20 D3
Coseley	Staffs	35 F5
Cosham	Hants	10 D4
Cotswold Hills	Glos	16D 1
Cottenham	Cambs	29 H1
Cottesmore	Rutl	37 E3
Cottingham	Yorks	51 E5
Coupar-Angus	Perth	73 E1
Coventry	Warks	35 H6
Coverack	Corn	2 D6
Cowbridge	Glam	15 E4
Cowdenbeath	Fife	73 E5
Cowes	I. of Wight	10 B5
Cowfold	Sussex	11 H3
Cowley	Oxon	18 A1
Cradley	Worcs	35 F5
Craggie	I'ness	81 G3
Craigellachie	Moray	82 C3
Craighouse	Jura	62 C2
Craignure	Mull	68 E4
Crail	Fife	73 H4
Cramond	M'loth	65 H1
Cranborne	Dorset	9 G3
Cranborne Chase	Dorset-Wilts	9 F3
Cranbrook	Kent	12 D3
Cranfield	Beds	28 D3
Cranleigh	Surrey	11 F1
Cranwell	Lincs	45 E6
Crathie Church	A'deen	76 C2
Craven Arms	Shrops	34 B6
Crawford	Lanark	65 F6
Crawley	Sussex	11 H2
Credenhill	Herefs	26 A3
Crediton	Devon	4 D1
Creetown	Kirkcud	57 E6
Cressage	Shrops	34 C4
Crewe	Ches	42 C5
Crewkerne	Som	8 C3
Crianlarich	Perth	71 E3
Criccieth	Caern	32 C1
Crickhowell	Brecon	25 G6
Cricklade	Wilts	17 E2
Crieff	Perth	71 C3
Crimond	A'deen	83 H2
Croft	Yorks	54 C4
Cromarty	Ross	81 G1
Cromdale	Moray	82 A4
Cromer	Norf	39 F1
Cromford	Derby	43 G5
Crooklands	W'land	53 E6
Crook of Alves	Moray	82 A1
Crook of Devon	Kinross	72 D4
Crosby	I. of Man	46 B5
Crosby	Lancs	41 H2
Crossford	Lanark	65 E4
Crossgates	Fife	73 E5
Cross Gates	Radn	25 F2
Cross Hands	Carm	12 B4
Crosshill	Ayr	56 D3
Crosshills	Yorks	48 C4
Cross-in-Hand	Sussex	12 B4
Crossway Green	Worcs	26 D1
Croston	Lancs	47 F6
Crowborough	Sussex	12 B4
Crowland	Lincs	37 G3
Crowle	Lincs	44 C1
Crown Hill	Devon	4 B5
Crowthorne	Berks	18 C5
Croxley Green	Herts	19 E2
Croyde	Devon	6 C2
Croydon	Surrey	19 G5
Cruden Bay	A'deen	83 H3
Crudgington	Shrops	34 C4
Crummock Water	Cumb	52 B3
Cuckfield	Sussex	11 H3
Cuckney	Notts	44 A4
Cudworth	Yorks	43 H1
Cuillin Hills	Skye	79 C6
Culbin Sandhills	Moray	81 H1
Cullen	Banff	82 D1
Cullingworth	Yorks	48 D4
Culloden Moor	I'ness	81 G3
Cullompton	Devon	5 F1
Culmstock	Devon	7 H4
Culross	Fife	72 D5
Culter	Lanark	65 G5
Cults	A'deen	77 H1
Culworth	Northants	28 B3
Culzean Castle	Ayr	63 H6
Cumberland, co.		52 C2
Cumbernauld	Dunb	65 E2
Cumnock	Ayr	56 F2
Cupar	Fife	73 F3
Currie	M'loth	65 H2
Cwmbran	Mon	15 G2
Dagenham	Essex	19 H3
Dalbeattie	Kirkcud	58 D5
Dalkeith	M'loth	66 A2
Dallas	Moray	82 A2
Dalmally	Argyll	70 D2
Dalmellington	Ayr	56 E3
Dalmeny	W. Loth	65 G1
Dalnaspidal	Perth	75 G4
Dalry	Ayr	64 A4
Dalry	Kirkcud	58 C3
Dalrymple	Ayr	56 D3
Dalston	Cumb	59 H6
Dalton	Dumf	59 F4
Dalton	Lancs	46 D1
Dalwhinnie	I'ness	75 F3
Darfield	Yorks	43 H1
Darlaston	Staffs	35 F4
Darlington	Durham	54 C3
Dartford	Kent	19 H4
Dartmoor	Devon	4 C3
Dartmouth	Devon	5 E5
Darvel	Ayr	64 C5
Darwen	Lancs	47 G5
Datchet	Bucks	19 E4
Daventry	Northants	28 B2
Dawlish	Devon	5 F3
Deal	Kent	13 H2
Dean, Forest of	Glos	16 B1
Dearham	Cumb	52 B2
Debden	Essex	30 A4
Debenham	Suff	31 F2
Deddington	Oxon	27 H4
Dee, R.	A'deen	77 G2
Deepcar	Yorks	43 G2
Deeping St. James	Lincs	37 F3
Delamere Forest	Ches	42 B4
Denbigh	Denb	41 F4
Denbighshire, co.		41 F5
Denham	Bucks	19 E3
Denholme	Yorks	48 D4
Dennington	Suff	31 G2
Denny	Stirl	65 E1
Denton	Lancs	43 E2
Deptford	Wilts	9 G1
Derby	Derby	36 A1
Derbyshire, co.		43 G4
Dervaig	Mull	68 C4
Derwen	Denb	41 G6
Desborough	Northants	36 D5
Devauden	Mon	16 A2
Devil's Beef Tub	Dumf	59 F1
Devil's Bridge	Card	33 E6
Devil's Elbow	Derby	43 E2
Devil's Elbow	Perth	76 C3
Devizes	Wilts	17 E5
Devon, co.		4 C1
Devonport	Devon	3 H3
Dewsbury	Yorks	49 E5
Diddlebury	Shrops	34 C5
Didmarton	Glos	16 C3
Digby	Lincs	45 E5
Dinas Mawddwy	Mer	33 F3
Dingwall	Ross	81 E2
Dirleton	E. Loth	66 C1
Dishforth	Yorks	49 F1
Diss	Norf	31 F1
Ditton Priors	Shrops	34 C5
Doddington	Cambs	37 H5
Doddington	N'land	67 G5
Dolgarrog	Caern	41 E4
Dolgellau	Mer	33 E3
Dollar	Clack	72 D4
Dolphinton	Lanark	65 G4
Dolwyddelan	Caern	40 D6
Doncaster	Yorks	44 B1
Donington	Lincs	37 G1
Dorchester	Dorset	8 D5
Dores	I'ness	81 F4
Dorking	Surrey	19 F6
Dornie	Ross	80 A5
Dornoch	Suth	87 B7
Dorset, co.		8 D4
Douglas	I. of Man	46 B5
Douglas	Lanark	65 E5
Doune	Perth	72 B4
Dounreay	Caith	86 C2
Dove Dale	Derby-Staffs	43 F5
Dover	Kent	13 H3
Dovercourt	Essex	31 F5
Dowally	Perth	76 B6
Dowlais	Glam	15 F1
Downham Market	Norf	38 B4
Downton	Hants	10 A5
Downton	Wilts	9 H2
Downtown	Devon	4 B2
Dreghorn	Ayr	64 B5
Drigg	Cumb	52 B5
Droitwich	Worcs	26 D2
Dronfield	Derby	43 H3
Drumbeg	Suth	84 B4
Drumelzier	Peebl	65 G5
Drumlithie	Kinc	77 G3
Drummore	Wig	57 B8
Drumnadrochit	I'ness	81 E4
Drumochter, Pass of	I'ness	75 G3
Dryburgh Abbey	Berwick	66 D5
Drymen	Stirl	64 C1
Drynoch	Skye	79 C5
Ducklington	Oxon	17 G1
Duddington	Northants	37 E4
Dudley	Worcs	35 F5
Duffield	Derby	36 A1
Dufftown	Banff	82 C3
Duich, Loch	Ross	80 A5
Dukeries, The	Notts	44 A3
Dukestown	Mon	15 F1
Dulnain Bridge	Moray	81 H4
Dumbarton	Dunb	64 B2
Dumfries	Dumf	59 E4
Dumfriesshire, co.		58 D3
Dunbar	E. Loth	66 D1
Dunbartonshire, co.		65 D2
Dunbeath	Caith	86 E4
Dunblane	Perth	72 B4
Duncansby	Caith	86 F1
Dunchurch	Warks	27 H1
Dundee	Angus	73 F2
Dundonald	Ayr	64 B5
Dundonnell	Ross	85 B7
Dundrennan	Kirkcud	58 D6
Dunfermline	Fife	73 E5
Dungeness	Kent	13 F5
Dunkeld	Perth	72 D1
Dunlop	Ayr	64 B4
Dunnet	Caith	86 E1
Dunning	Perth	72 D3
Dunnottar Castle	Kinc	77 H3
Dunoon	Argyll	63 H1
Duns	Berwick	67 E3
Dunscore	Dumf	58 D3
Dunsfold	Surrey	11 F2
Dunsop Bridge	Yorks	47 G3
Dunstable	Beds	29 E5
Dunstaffnage Castle	Argyll	70 B2
Dunster	Som	7 G1
Dunsyre	Lanark	65 G4
Duntulm	Skye	78 C2
Dunvegan	Skye	78 A4
Durham	Durham	54 C1
Durham, co.		54 A1
Durness	Suth	84 D2
Durnford	Wilts	9 H1
Dursley	Glos	16 C2
Durston	Som	8 B2
Duthil	I'ness	81 H5
Duxford	Cambs	29 H3
Dyce	A'deen	83 G5
Dyffryn	Mer	32 D2
Dymchurch	Kent	13 F4
Dymock	Herefs	26 C4
Dysart	Fife	73 F5
Eaglesfield	Dumf	59 G4
Eaglesham	Renf	64 C4
Ealing	Middx	19 F3
Eardisley	Herefs	25 G3
Earith	Hunts	29 G1
Earlestown	Lancs	42 B2
Earls Colne	Essex	30 C5
Earlsferry	Fife	73 G4
Earl Shilton	Leics	36 A4
Earlston	Berwick	66 D4
Earn, Loch	Perth	72 A3
Earsdon	N'land	61 G4
Easebourne	Sussex	11 E3
Easington	Durham	54 C1
Easingwold	Yorks	49 G2
Eastbourne	Sussex	12 C6
East Cowes	I. of Wight	10 C5
East Dereham	Norf	38 D3
East Grinstead	Sussex	12 A3
East Ham	Essex	20 B3
East Harling	Norf	39 E6
Eastington	Glos	16 C1
East Kilbride	Lanark	64 D3
Eastleigh	Hants	10 B3
East Linton	E. Loth	66 D1
East Lothian, co.		66 C2
East Markham	Notts	44 C4
East Retford	Notts	44 B3
East Riding, div.	Yorks	50 D3
Eastry	Kent	13 H2
East Wemyss	Fife	73 F5
Eaton	Norf	39 F4
Eaton Socon	Beds	29 F2
Ebbw Vale	Mon	15 F1
Ebchester	Durham	61 F5
Ecclefechan	Dumf	59 G4
Eccles	Berwick	67 E4
Eccles	Lancs	42 C2
Ecclesfield	Yorks	43 H2
Eccleshall	Staffs	35 E2
Echt	A'deen	77 G1
Eckford	Rox	66 D5
Eckington	Derby	43 H3
Eddleston	Peebl	66 A4
Edenbridge	Kent	12 B2
Edgbaston	Warks	35 F5
Edgware	Middx	19 F2
Edinburgh	M'loth	65 H2
Edlingham	N'land	61 F1
Edmondbyers	Durham	61 E6
Edmonton	Middx	19 G2
Edzell	Angus	77 F4
Egham	Surrey	19 E4
Eglingham	N'land	67 G6
Egmanton	Notts	44 C4
Egremont	Cumb	52 A4
Egton	Yorks	55 F4
Eil, Loch	I'ness	74 B4
Eilean, Loch an	I'ness	81 H6
Elderslie	Renf	64 C3
Elgin	Moray	82 B1
Elgol	Skye	79 D7
Elie	Fife	73 G4
Elland	Yorks	48 D6
Ellesmere	Shrops	34 B1
Ellesmere Port	Ches	42 A4
Ellington	N'land	61 G3
Ellon	A'deen	83 G4
Ellsley	Berks	17 H3
Elmdon	Warks	35 G5
Elphin	Suth	85 C6
Elrick	A'deen	83 F6
Elsdon	N'land	61 E2
Elstree	Herts	19 F2
Eltham	London	19 H4
Elvington	Yorks	50 C3
Ely	Cambs	38 A6
Embleton	N'land	67 9H
Empingham	Rutl	37 E4
Emsworth	Hants	10 D4
Enard B.	Ross	85 A5
Enfield	Middx	20 A2
Ennerdale Water	Cumb	52 B3
Epping	Essex	19 H2
Epping Forest		20 B2
Epsom	Surrey	19 F5
Epworth	Lincs	44 C1
Erdington	Warks	35 G5
Eriboll, Loch	Suth	84 D2
Ericht, Loch	I'ness	75 F4
Eriskay, I.	I'ness	88 E3
Erith	Kent	19 H4
Ermine Street	Lincs	44 D3
Errol	Perth	73 F2
Erskine Ferry	Dunb-Renf	64 C2
Esher	Surrey	19 F5
Eskdale	Cumb	52 C4
Essex, co.		20 C1
Eston	Yorks	54 D3
Etive, Loch	Argyll	70 C2
Eton	Bucks	18 D4
Ettington	Warks	27 G3
Ettrick Church	Selk	66 A6
Euston	Suff	38 D6
Evanton	Ross	81 F1
Evesham	Worcs	27 E3
Evesham, Vale of	Worcs	27 E3
Ewe, Loch	Ross	78 F1
Ewell	Surrey	19 F5
Exeter	Devon	5 E2
Exmoor	Som-Devon	7 E1
Exmouth	Devon	5 F3
Eyam	Derby	43 G3
Eye	Suff	31 F1
Eyemouth	Berwick	67 F2
Eynort, Loch	S. Uist	88 E3
Eynsford	Kent	20 B5
Fairford	Glos	17 F2
Fairlie	Ayr	63 H2
Fairmilehead	M'loth	66 A2
Fair Oak	Hants	10 C3
Fakenham	Norf	38 D2
Falkirk	Stirl	72 C6
Falkland	Fife	73 F4
Falmouth	Corn	2 D5
Falstone	N'land	60 C3
Fannich, Loch	Ross	80 C2
Fareham	Hants	10 C4
Faringdon	Berks	17 G2
Farnborough	Hants	18 D6
Farne Is.	N'land	67 H4
Farnham	Surrey	18 C6
Farningham	Kent	20 C5
Farnsfield	Notts	44 B5
Farnworth	Lancs	42 C1
Farrington Gurney	Som	16 B5
Farsley	Yorks	49 E4
Faversham	Kent	13 F1
Fearn	Ross	87 B8
Felixstowe	Suff	31 G4
Felling	Durham	61 G5
Feltham	Middx	19 E4
Felton	N'land	61 F2
Feltwell	Norf	38 B5
Fenny Stratford	Bucks	28 D4
Fenwick	Ayr	64 C4
Fern Down	Dorset	9 G4
Fernhurst	Sussex	11 E2
Ferrybridge	Yorks	50 A5
Ferryden	Angus	77 G5
Fettercairn	Kinc	77 F4
Ffestiniog	Mer	33 E1
Fforestfach	Glam	14 C2
Fife, co.		73 F4
Filey	Yorks	51 F1
Filton	Glos	16 B3
Finchingfield	Essex	30 B4
Finchley	Middx	19 F3
Findhorn	Moray	82 A1
Findochty	Banff	82 D1
Findon	Kinc	77 H2
Findon	Sussex	11 G4
Finningham	Suff	31 E2
Finningley	Notts	44 B2
Fishguard	Pemb	22 B2
Fittleworth	Sussex	11 F3
Flamborough Hd.	Yorks	51 G2
Fleet	Hants	18 C6
Fleetwood	Lancs	46 D3
Fletching	Sussex	12 B4
Flimby	Cumb	52 A2
Flint	Flint	41 H4
Flintshire, co.		41 G4
Flockton	Yorks	49 E6
Flodden Field	N'land	67 F5
Flookburg	Lancs	47 E1
Fochabers	Moray	82 C2
Folkestone	Kent	13 G3
Folkingham	Lincs	37 F2
Fordingbridge	Hants	9 H3

Fordwich Kettewell

Fordwich Kent 13 G2
Forfar Angus 77 E5
Formby Lancs 41 H1
Forres Moray 82 A2
Fort Augustus I'ness 74 D1
Fort George I'ness 81 G2
Forth Br. 65 G1
Forth, R. 72 C5
Fortingall Perth 75 G6
Fortrose Ross 81 F2
Fortuneswell Dorset 9 E6
Fort William I'ness 74 C4
Foss Way Notts 36 C3
Foulness I. Essex 21 F3
Fountains Abbey Yorks 49 E2
Four Crosses Caern 32 B1
Fowey Corn 3 F3
Foyers I'ness 81 E5
Framlingham Suff 31 G2
Frampton Cotterell Glos 16 B3
Frant Sussex 12 C3
Fraserburgh A'deen 83 H1
Freckleton Lancs 47 E5
Freshwater I. of Wight 10 B5
Fressingfield Suff 31 F1
Freswick Caith 86 F1
Frinton Essex 31 F6
Friockheim Angus 77 F5
Fritham Hants 10 A3
Frizington W'land 52 A3
Frodsham Ches 42 B3
Frome Som 16 C6
Fulford Yorks 50 B3
Fulwood Lancs 47 F5
Fyne, Loch Argyll 70 B5
Fyvie A'deen 83 F3
Gailey Staffs 35 E3
Gainsborough Lincs 44 C2
Gairloch Ross 78 F2
Galashiels Selk 66 C5
Galgate Lancs 47 F3
Galloway 57 C6
Galston Ayr 64 C5
Gamlingay Cambs 29 F3
Gamston Notts 44 B3
Garboldisham Norf 39 E6
Garelochhead Dunb 70 D5
Garforth Yorks 49 F4
Gargunnock Stirl 72 B5
Garlieston Wig 57 E7
Garmouth Moray 82 C1
Garry, Loch I'ness 74 D2
Garstang Lancs 47 F4
Garston Lancs 42 A3
Garth Brecon 25 E3
Garthmyl Mont 33 H4
Garton-on-the-Wolds Yorks 51 E2
Garvald E. Loth 66 D2
Garve Ross 80 D2
Garynahine Lewis 88 B2
Gateacre Lancs 42 A3
Gatehouse-of-Fleet Kirkcud 58 C5
Gateshead Durham 61 G5
Gatwick Airport Surrey 11 H1
Gerrards Cross Bucks 18 D3
Gifford E. Loth 66 C2
Gilfach Glam 15 F2
Gillingham Dorset 9 E2
Gillingham Kent 20 D4
Gilsland Cumb 60 C4
Girvan Ayr 55 B4
Gisburn Yorks 47 H3
Glamis Angus 73 F1
Glamorganshire, co. 14 D2
Glascarnoch Res. Ross 80 C1
Glasgow Lanark 64 C2
Glas Maol, mt. Angus 76 C3
Glass Houghton Yorks 49 F5
Glastonbury Som 8 C1
Glen Affric I'ness 80 C5
Glen Almond Perth 72 B2
Glenboig Lanark 64 D2
Glenbuck Ayr 65 E5
Glen Coe Argyll 74 C5
Glendevon Perth 72 D4
Gleneagles Perth 72 C3
Glenelg I'ness 79 F6
Glenfarg Perth 73 E3
Glenfinnan I'ness 74 A3
Glen Garry Perth 74 C2
Glenisla Angus 76 C5
Glenluce Wig 57 C7
Glen Lyon Perth 74 C1
Glen Moriston I'ness 80 C6
Glenridding W'land 52 D3
Glenrothes Fife 73 F4
Glen Shee Perth 76 B4
Glen Shiel Ross 80 A6
Glen Trool Kirkcud 57 D5
Glossop Derby 43 E2
Gloucester Glos 26 C5
Gloucestershire, co. 26 C6
Glyncorrwg Glam 14 D2
Glyndebourne Sussex 12 B5
Glyn Neath Glam 14 D1
Goat Fell, mt. Arran 63 F3
Goathland Yorks 55 F4
Godalming Surrey 18 D6
Godmanchester Hunts 29 F1
Godshill I. of Wight 10 C6
Golcar Yorks 48 D6
Golden Valley Herefs 25 H4
Golspie Suth 87 B6
Gomersal Yorks 49 E5
Goodwick Pemb 22 B2
Goole Yorks 49 H5
Gordonstown A'deen 82 F3
Gordonstown Banff 82 D2
Gorebridge M'loth 66 B3
Goring Oxon 18 B3
Goring Sussex 11 G5
Gorleston Norf 39 H4
Gorseinon Glam 14 B2
Gosforth Cumb 52 B4
Gosforth N'land 61 G4
Gosport Hants 10 C4
Gourock Renf 63 H1
Govan Lanark 64 C2
Gower Pen. Glam 14 E3
Gowerton Glam 14 B2
Grampound Corn 3 E3
Grange Lancs 47 E1
Grangemill Derby 43 G5
Grangemouth Stirl 64 F1
Grantchester Cambs 29 H2
Grantham Lincs 37 E1
Granton M'loth 65 H1
Grantown-on-Spey Moray 82 A4
Grant's House Berwick 67 E2
Grasmere W'land 52 D4
Gravesend Kent 20 C4
Grayshott Hants 11 F2
Grays Thurrock Essex 20 C4
Great Ayton Yorks 55 E4
Great Casterton Rutl 37 E3
Great Chesterford Essex 30 A3
Great Cumbrae, I. Bute 63 H2
Great Driffield Yorks 51 E3
Great Dunmow Essex 30 B5
Great Gidding Hunts 37 F6
Greatham Durham 54 D2
Greatham Hants 11 E2
Great Harwood Lancs 47 G5
Great Limber Lincs 45 E1
Great Malvern Worcs 26 C3
Great Missenden Bucks 18 D2
Great Orton Cumb 59 H5
Great Salkeld Cumb 53 E2
Great Shefford Berks 17 G4
Great Shelford Cambs 30 A3
Great Staughton Hunts 29 F2
Great Torrington Devon 6 D3
Great Wakering Essex 21 E3
Great Waltham Essex 20 D1
Great Witley Worcs 26 C1
Great Yarmouth Norf 39 H4
Greenfield Flint 41 G4
Greenhead N'land 60 C5
Greenhithe Kent 20 C4
Greenlaw Berwick 66 D4
Greenock Renf 63 H1
Greenwich London 19 G4
Gretna Dumf 59 G4
Gretna Green Dumf 59 G4
Greystoke Cumb 52 D2
Griffithstown Mon 15 G2
Grimsby Lincs 45 G1
Gringley-on-the-Hill Notts 44 C2
Gronant Flint 40 G3
Groombridge Sussex 12 B3
Gruinard B. Ross 85 A7
Guildford Surrey 19 E6
Guisborough Yorks 55 E3
Guiseley Yorks 48 D4
Gullane E. Loth 66 C1
Gunnislake Corn 3 H1
Gunwalloe Corn 2 C6
Guyhirne Cambs 37 H4
Gwalchmai Angl 40 B4
Gwbert Card 22 D1
Gweek Corn 2 C5
Gwithian Corn 2 B4
Gwyddgrug Carm 23 F2
Gyffylliog Denb 41 F5
Hackthorpe W'land 53 E3
Haddenham Bucks 18 C1
Haddenham Cambs 29 H1
Haddington E. Loth 66 D2
Haddiscoe Norf 29 H5
Hadleigh Suff 31 E4
Hailsham Sussex 12 C5
Hale Lancs 42 A3
Halesowen Worcs 35 F5
Halesworth Suff 31 G1
Halfway Brecon 24 D4
Halifax Yorks 48 D5
Halkirk Caith 86 D2
Hallsands Devon 5 E6
Halstead Essex 30 C5
Haltwhistle N'land 60 C5
Halwell Devon 4 D5
Hamble Hants 10 B4
Hambleden Bucks 18 C3
Hambledon Hants 10 D3
Hambledon Surrey 11 F2
Hambleton Hills Yorks 54 D5
Hamilton Lanark 64 D3
Hampshire, co. 10 B2
Hampstead London 19 F3
Hampton Middx 19 F4
Hampton-in-Arden Warks 35 G6
Ham Street Kent 13 F4
Hanbury Worcs 26 D2
Handcross Sussex 11 H2
Handsworth Yorks 43 H3
Hanley Staffs 42 D6
Hanworth Middx 19 E4
Happisburgh Norf 39 G2
Harbury Warks 27 G2
Harby Leics 36 C2
Harewood Yorks 49 E4
Harlech Mer 32 D2
Harleston Norf 39 F6
Harlow Essex 20 B1
Harpenden Herts 18 E1
Harrington Cumb 52 A3
Harris I'ness 88 A3
Harrogate Yorks 49 E3
Harrow-on-the-Hill Middx 19 F3
Harston Cambs 29 H3
Hartburn N'land 61 F3
Hartfield Sussex 12 B3
Harthill Ches 42 B5
Harthill Lanark 65 F2
Hartington Derby 43 F5
Hartland Devon 6 B3
Hartlepool Durham 54 D2
Harwell Berks 18 A3
Harwich Essex 31 F5
Haslemere Surrey 11 E2
Haslingden Lancs 47 H5
Hastings Sussex 12 D5
Haswell Durham 54 C1
Hatfield Herts 19 F1
Hatfield Yorks 44 B1
Hatfield Broad Oak Essex 30 A6
Hatfield Peverel Essex 30 C6
Hatherleigh Devon 6 D4
Hathern Leics 36 B2
Hathersage Derby 43 G3
Hatton A'deen 83 H3
Havant Hants 10 D4
Haverfordwest Pemb 22 C4
Haverhill Suff 30 B3
Haverton Hill Durham 54 D3
Hawarden Flint 41 H4
Hawes Water W'land 53 E3
Hawick Rox 60 B1
Hawkshead Lancs 52 D5
Hawkstone Park Shrops 34 C2
Haworth Yorks 48 C4
Haxey Lincs 44 C2
Haydon Bridge N'land 60 D5
Hayes Middx 19 E3
Hayfield Derby 43 E3
Hayle Corn 2 B4
Hayling I. Hants 10 D4
Hay-on-Wye Brecon 25 G4
Hayton Yorks 50 C4
Haywards Heath Sussex 12 A4
Hazel Grove Ches 43 E3
Headington Oxon 28 A6
Headless Cross Worcs 27 E2
Heanor Derby 43 H6
Heapham Lincs 44 D3
Heaton Park Lancs 42 D1
Hebden Bridge Yorks 48 C5
Heckington Lincs 37 F1
Heckmondwike Yorks 48 D5
Heddon-on-the-Wall N'land 61 F5
Hednesford Staffs 35 F3
Hedon Yorks 51 F5
Helensburgh Dunb 64 A1
Helmdon Northants 28 B3
Helmsdale Suth 87 D5
Helmsley Yorks 55 E6
Helston Corn 2 C5
Helvellyn, mt. Cumb 52 D3
Hemel Hempstead Herts 18 E1
Hemswell Lincs 44 D2
Hendon Middx 19 F3
Hendy Glam 23 G5
Henfield Sussex 11 H3
Henley-in-Arden Warks 27 F1
Henley-on-Thames Oxon 18 C3
Henstridge Som 9 E3
Hereford Herefs 26 A3
Herefordshire, co. 25 H3
Heriot M'loth 66 B3
Herne Bay Kent 13 G1
Hertford Herts 19 G1
Hertfordshire, co. 29 E6
Herriard Hants 18 B6
Herstmonceux Sussex 12 C5
Hesketh Bank Lancs 47 E5
Hethersett Norf 39 F4
Hetton-le-Hole Durham 61 H6
Hexham N'land 61 E5
Heyford, Upr. & Lr. Oxon 28 A5
Heysham Lancs 47 E2
Heytesbury Wilts 16 D6
Heywood Lancs 42 D1
Higham Derby 43 H5
Higham Ferrers Northants 29 E1
High Bentham Yorks 47 G2
Highbridge Som 15 G6
Highgate Middx 19 F3
High Halden Kent 13 E3
High Ongar Essex 20 C2
Highworth Wilts 17 F2
High Wycombe Bucks 18 D2
Hilderstone Staffs 35 F1
Hillington Lanark 64 C3
Hillington Norf 38 C2
Hill of Fearn Ross 87 B8
Hillside Kinc 77 F5
Hinckley Leics 36 A5
Hinderwell Yorks 55 F3
Hindhead Surrey 10 E2
Hindley Lancs 42 B1
Hindon Wilts 9 F1
Hingham Norf 39 E4
Hirwaun Glam 15 E1
Hitchin Herts 29 F5
Hobkirk Rox 60 B1
Hockering Norf 39 E3
Hockley Heath Warks 27 F1
Hoddesdon Herts 20 A1
Hodnet Shrops 34 C2
Hogs Back Surrey 11 F1
Holbeach Lincs 37 H2
Holland, div. Lincs 37 G2
Hollington Derby 43 G6
Holmbury St. Mary Surrey 11 G1
Holme-on-Spalding-Moor Yorks 50 C4
Holmes Chapel Ches 42 D4
Holmesfield Derby 43 G3
Holmfirth Yorks 43 F1
Holmwood Surrey 19 F6
Holsworthy Devon 6 C4
Holt Denb 42 A5
Holt Norf 39 E1
Holy I. N'land 67 G4
Holyhead Angl 40 A3
Holywell Flint 41 G4
Honington Suff 38 D6
Honiton Devon 5 G1
Hope-under-Dinmore Herefs 26 A2
Horbury Yorks 49 E6
Horeb Card 24 A4
Horley Surrey 11 H1
Horncastle Lincs 45 F4
Hornchurch Essex 20 B3
Horndean Hants 10 D3
Hornsea Yorks 51 F3
Hornsey Middx 19 G3
Horsebridge Hants 10 B2
Horsebridge Sussex 12 C5
Horsforth Yorks 49 E4
Horsham Sussex 11 G2
Horsham St. Faith Norf 39 F3
Horwich Lancs 42 C1
Houghton Hunts 29 G1
Houghton-le-Spring Durham 61 H6
Hounslow Middx 19 E4
Hove Sussex 11 H4
Howden Yorks 49 H5
Howwood Renf 64 B3
Hoy, I. Orkney 89 A7
Hoylake Ches 41 G3
Hucknall Notts 44 A6
Huddersfield Yorks 48 D6
Huggate Yorks 50 D3
Hull Yorks 51 E5
Hullavington Wilts 16 D3
Humshaugh N'land 61 E4
Hungerford Berks 17 G4
Hunmanby Yorks 51 E1
Huntingdon Hunts 29 F1
Huntingdonshire, co. 37 F6
Huntly A'deen 82 D3
Hurlford Ayr 64 C5
Hurn Hants 9 H4
Hursley Hants 10 B2
Hurst Green Sussex 12 D4
Hurstpierpoint Sussex 11 H3
Husbands Bosworth Leics 36 C5
Hutton-le-Hole Yorks 55 E5
Huyton Lancs 42 A3
Hyde Ches 43 E2
Hythe Hants 10 B4
Hythe Kent 13 G3
Ibsley Hants 9 H3
Ickenham Middx 19 E3
Idle Yorks 48 D4
Ilchester Som 8 C2
Ilford Essex 19 H3
Ilfracombe Devon 6 D1
Ilkeston Derby 36 B1
Ilkley Yorks 48 D3
Ilminster Som 8 B3
Immingham Dock Lincs 51 F6
Inchcolm Fife 73 E6
Inchkeith Fife 73 F6
Inchnadamph Suth 85 C5
Ingatestone Essex 20 C2
Ingleby Cross Yorks 54 D5
Ingleton Yorks 47 G1
Ingoldmells Lincs 45 H4
Innellan Argyll 63 G1
Innerleithen Peebl 66 B5
Insch A'deen 83 E4
Inverallochy A'deen 83 H1
Inveran Suth 85 F6
Inveraray Argyll 70 C4
Inverbervie Kinc 77 G4
Invercassley Suth 85 E6
Inveresk M'loth 66 B2
Inverfarigaig I'ness 81 E5
Invergarry I'ness 74 D2
Invergordon Ross 81 F1
Inverkeilor Angus 77 G5
Inverkeithing Fife 73 E6
Inverkirkaig Suth 85 B5
Invermoriston I'ness 80 D5
Inverness I'ness 81 F3
Inverness-shire, co. 74 B2
Invershiel Ross 80 A5
Invershin Suth 85 F6
Inverurie A'deen 83 F4
Iona, I. Argyll 69 B6
Ipstones Staffs 43 E6
Ipswich Suff 31 F4
Irlam Lancs 42 C2
Ironbridge Shrops 34 D4
Irthington Cumb 60 B5
Irthlingborough Northants 28 D1
Irvine Ayr 64 B5
Islay, I. Argyll 62 A2
Isle of Ely, div. Cambs 37 H5
Isle of Man 46 A4
Isle of Wight Hants 10 B6
Isle Ornsay Skye 79 E7
Itchen Hants 10 B4
Iver Bucks 19 E3
Ivybridge Devon 4 C5
Ixworth Suff 30 D1
Jameston Pemb 22 C5
Jamestown Dunb 64 B1
Janetstown Caith 86 D2
Janetstown Caith 86 E4
Jarrow Durham 61 G5
Jedburgh Rox 66 D6
Jodrellbank Ches 42 D4
John o' Groats Caith 86 F1
Johnshaven Kinc 77 G4
Johnstone Renf 64 B3
Jura, I. Argyll 62 C1
Jurby I. of Man 46 B4
Katrine, Loch Perth 71 E4
Keighley Yorks 48 C4
Keiss Caith 86 F2
Keith Banff 82 D2
Kelsall Ches 42 B4
Kelso Rox 67 E5
Kelty Fife 73 E5
Kelvedon Essex 30 D6
Kemble Glos 17 E2
Kempsey Worcs 26 D3
Kendal W'land 53 E5
Kenilworth Warks 27 G1
Kenley Surrey 12 A1
Kenmore Perth 75 H6
Kenninghall Norf 39 E6
Kennoway Fife 73 F4
Kent, co 12 D2
Kentford Suff 30 C2
Kenton Devon 5 E2
Kerrera, I. Argyll 70 A2
Kessingland Suff 39 H6
Kessock, N. Ross 81 F3
Kessock, S. I'ness 81 F3
Kesteven, div. Lincs 36 D1
Keswick Cumb 52 C3
Kettering Northants 36 D6
Kettewell Yorks 48 C1

Kew Gardens Mexborough

Kew Gardens Surrey 19 F4
Keynsham Som 16 B5
Kidderminster Worcs 35 E6
Kidlington Oxon 18 A1
Kidwelly Carm 14 A1
Kilbarchan Renf 64 B3
Kilbirnie Ayr 64 B3
Kilchoan Argyll 68 C3
Kilconquhar Fife 73 G4
Kilcreggan Dunb 70 D6
Kildrummy A'deen 82 D5
Kilfinan Argyll 70 B6
Kilkhampton Corn 6 B4
Killearn Stirl 64 C1
Killiecrankie, Pass of Perth 76 A4
Killin Perth 72 A2
Killinaig Mull 69 D5
Killinghall Yorks 49 E2
Kilmacolm Renf 64 B2
Kilmaluig Skye 78 C2
Kilmarnock Ayr 64 B5
Kilmartin Argyll 70 A5
Kilmaurs Ayr 64 B4
Kilmelfort Argyll 69 F6
Kilmichael Argyll 70 B5
Kilmory Argyll 69 D2
Kilmory Arran 63 F5
Kilmuir Ross 87 A8
Kilninver Argyll 70 A3
Kilpatrick Hills Dunb 64 B2
Kilrenny Fife 73 H4
Kilsyth Stirl 64 D1
Kilwinning Ayr 64 B4
Kimbolton Hunts 29 E1
Kinbrace Suth 86 B4
Kincardine-on-Forth Fife 72 C5
Kincardine O'Neil A'deen 77 F1
Kincardineshire, co. 77 F3
Kincraig I'ness 75 H1
Kineton Warks 27 G3
Kinghorn Fife 73 E5
Kingsand Corn 3 H3
Kingsbarns Fife 73 H3
Kingsbridge Devon 4 D6
Kingsburgh Skye 78 B4
Kingsbury Warks 35 H4
Kingsclere Hants 18 A5
Kings Cliffe Northants 37 E4
Kingshouse Argyll 74 D5
Kingskettle Fife 73 F4
King's Langley Herts 18 E2
King's Lynn Norf 38 B3
Kings Somborne Hants 10 B2
Kingsteignton Devon 5 E3
Kingsthorpe Northants 28 C2
Kingston Surrey 19 F4
Kingston Bagpuize Berks 17 H2
Kingswear Devon 5 E5
Kingswood Glos 16 B4
Kings Worthy Hants 10 B2
Kington Herefs 25 G2
Kingussie I'ness 75 G2
Kinloch Bervie Suth 84 C2
Kinlochewe Ross 80 B2
Kinloch Hourn I'ness 74 B1
Kinlochleven Argyll 74 C5
Kinlochmoidart I'ness 68 E2
Kinloch Rannoch Perth 75 G5
Kinloss Moray 82 A1
Kinneff Kinc 77 H3
Kinross Kinross 73 E4
Kinross-shire, co. 72 D4
Kintore A'deen 83 F5
Kintyre, Mull of Argyll 62 D6
Kirby Hill Yorks 49 F2
Kirkbride Cumb 59 G5
Kirkby-in-Ashfield Notts 44 A5
Kirkby Lonsdale W'land 47 F1
Kirkbymoorside Yorks 55 E6
Kirkby Stephen W'land 53 G4
Kirkcaldy Fife 73 F5
Kirkcolm Wig 57 A6
Kirkconnel Dumf 58 C1
Kirkcowan Wig 58 A5
Kirkcudbright Kirkcud 58 C6
Kirkcudbrightshire, co. 58 B4
Kirkfieldbank Lanark 65 E4
Kirkham Lancs 47 E5
Kirkheaton Yorks 48 D6
Kirkintilloch Dunb 64 D2
Kirkmaiden Wig 57 B8
Kirkmichael Ayr 56 D3
Kirk Michael Isle of Man 46 B4
Kirkmichael Perth 76 B5
Kirknewton M'loth 65 G2
Kirknewton N'land 67 F5
Kirk of Mochrum Wig 57 D7
Kirkoswald Ayr 56 C3
Kirkoswald Cumb 53 E1
Kirkpatrick Dumf 59 G4
Kirksanton Cumb 46 C1
Kirkton of Rayne A'deen 83 E4
Kirkwall Orkney 89 B6
Kirk Yetholm Rox 67 E5
Kirn Argyll 64 A2
Kirriemuir Angus 76 D5
Kirton Lincs 37 G1
Kirton-in-Lindsey Lincs 44 D2
Knaresborough Yorks 49 F3
Knarsdale N'land 60 C6
Knighton Radn 25 G1
Knockandhu Banff 82 B4
Knottingley Yorks 50 A5
Knutsford Ches 42 D3
Kyleakin Skye 79 E6
Kylerhea Skye 79 F6
Kylesku Suth 84 C4
Lacock Wilts 16 D4
Ladybank Fife 73 F3
Laggan I'ness 75 F2
Laggan, Loch I'ness 75 E3
Lairg Suth 85 F6
Lakenheath Suff 38 C5
Lambourn Berks 17 G3
Lamington Lanark 65 F5
Lamlash Arran 63 G4
Lammermuir Hills 66 C3
Lampeter Card 24 B3
Lanark Lanark 65 F4
Lanarkshire, co. 65 E4
Lancashire, co. 47 F6
Lancaster Lancs 47 F2
Lanchester Durham 61 F6
Land's End Corn 2 A5
Langdale W'land 52 C4
Langford Beds 29 F4
Langholm Dumf 60 A3
Langport Som 8 C2
Langwathby Cumb 53 E2
Lapford Devon 7 E4
Larbert Stirl 64 E1
Largo Fife 73 G4
Largo Ward Fife 73 G4
Largs Ayr 63 H2
Larkhall Lanark 65 E4
Lasswade M'loth 66 B2
Lastingham Yorks 55 F5
Latchingdon Essex 21 E2
Latheron Caith 86 E4
Lauder Berwick 66 C4
Laugharne Carm 23 E4
Launceston Corn 4 A2
Laurencekirk Kinc 77 G4
Lavenham Suff 30 D3
Laxey Isle of Man 46 C5
Laxfield Suff 31 G1
Laxford Bridge Suth 84 C3
Laxton Notts 44 C4
Lazonby Cumb 53 E1
Leadenham Lincs 44 D5
Leaden Roding Essex 30 B6
Leadhills Dumf 58 D1
Leamington Spa Warks 27 G1
Leatherhead Surrey 19 F5
Lechlade Glos 17 F2
Ledbury Herefs 26 C4
Leeds Yorks 49 E5
Leek Staffs 43 E5
Leeming Yorks 54 C5
Leicester Leics 36 B4
Leicestershire, co. 36 A3
Leigh Lancs 42 C2
Leigh Surrey 19 F6
Leigh-on-Sea Essex 20 D3
Leighterton Glos 16 C3
Leighton Buzzard Beds 28 D5
Leintwardine Herefs 25 H1
Leiston Suff 31 H2
Leith M'loth 65 H1
Lendalfoot Ayr 56 B4
Lennoxtown Stirl 64 D1
Leny, Pass of Perth 71 G4
Lenzie Dunb 64 D2
Leominster Herefs 26 A2
Lerwick Shet 89 E7
Lesbury N'land 61 G1
Leslie Fife 73 F4
Lesmahagow Lanark 65 E4
Letchworth Herts 29 F4
Letham Angus 77 E6
Leuchars Fife 73 G3
Leven Fife 73 G4
Leven, Loch Argyll/I'ness 74 C5
Leven, Loch Kinross 73 E4
Levenshulme Lancs 42 D2
Lewes Sussex 12 B5
Lewis Ross 88 A2
Leyburn Yorks 54 A5
Leyland Lancs 47 F5
Leyton Essex 19 G3
Liberton M'loth 66 A2
Lichfield Staffs 35 G3
Lifton Devon 4 A2
Lilliesleaf Rox 66 C6
Lincoln Lincs 44 D4
Lincolnshire, co. 44 D5
Lincoln Wolds Lincs 45 F2
Lindisfarne I. N'land 67 G4
Lindsey, div. Lincs 44 D3
Lingen Herefs 25 H2
Lingfield Surrey 12 A2
Linlithgow W. Loth 65 F1
Linnhe, Loch Argyll/I'ness 74 B5
Linslade Bucks 28 D5
Linthwaite Yorks 48 D6
Linton Cambs 30 A3
Linton-upon-Ouse Yorks 49 G2
Liphook Hants 11 E2
Liskeard Corn 3 G3
Lismore, I. Argyll 70 A2
Liss Hants 10 D2
Littleborough Lancs 48 C6
Littlebury Essex 30 A4
Little Cheverell Wilts 17 E6
Little Dean Glos 16 B1
Littlehampton Sussex 11 F5
Littleport Cambs 38 A5
Little Rissington Glos 27 F5
Little Snoring Norf 38 D2
Littlestone Kent 13 F4
Liverpool Lancs 42 A2
Liversedge Yorks 48 D5
Lizard Pt. Corn 2 C6
Llanaelhaiarn Caern 32 B1
Llanallgo Angl 40 C3
Llanarth Card 24 A3
Llanbedrog Caern 32 B2
Llanberis Caern 40 C5
Llanbister Radn 25 F1
Llanbydder Carm 24 B4
Llandaff Glam 15 F4
Llanddarog Carm 24 B6
Llanddeiniolen Caern 40 C5
Llandderfel Mer 33 F1
Llandefeilog Carm 23 F4
Llandilo Carm 23 G3
Llandinam Mont 33 G5
Llandissilio Pemb 22 D4
Llandovery Carm 23 H2
Llandrillo Mer 33 G1
Llandrindod Wells Radn 25 F2
Llandudno Caern 41 E3
Llandybie Carm 23 G4
Llandyssul Card 23 F2
Llanelltyd Mer 33 E3
Llanelly Glam 14 B2
Llanerchymedd Angl 40 B3
Llanerfyl Mont 33 G3
Llanfaethlu Angl 40 A3
Llanfair Caereinion Mont 33 G4
Llanfairfechan Caern 40 D4
Llanfairpwllgwyngyll Angl 40 C4
Llanfair Talhaiarn Denb 41 F4
Llanfarian Card 24 B1
Llanfihangel-ar-arth Carm 23 F2
Llanfihangel Glyn Myfyr Denb 41 F6
Llanfihangel Ystrad Card 24 B3
Llanfyllin Mont 33 H3
Llanfynydd Carm 23 G3
Llangadog Carm 24 C5
Llangarren Herefs 26 A5
Llangefni Angl 40 B4
Llangelynin Mer 32 D4
Llangernyw Denb 41 E4
Llangoed Angl 40 C3
Llangollen Denb 33 H1
Llangranog Card 22 E1
Llangrove Herefs 26 A5
Llangunllo Radn 25 G1
Llangurig Mont 33 F6
Llangynog Mont 33 G2
Llanidloes Mont 33 F5
Llanilar Card 24 B1
Llanllwni Carm 23 F2
Llanrhystyd Card 24 B2
Llanrwst Denb 41 E5
Llansannan Denb 41 F5
Llansawel Carm 24 C4
Llantrisant Glam 15 F3
Llantwit Major Glam 15 E4
Llanuwchllyn Mer 33 F2
Llanwrda Carm 23 H3
Llanwrtyd Wells Brecon 24 D3
Llanyre Radn 25 E2
Llechryd Card 22 D2
Llyswen Brecon 25 F4
Loanhead M'loth 66 A2
Lopcombe Corner Wilts 10 A2
Lochaline Argyll 68 E4
Lochalsh, Kyle of Ross 79 F6
Lochboisdale S. Uist 88 E3
Lochbuie Mull 69 E5
Lochcarron Ross 80 A4
Lochdonhead Mull 69 E5
Lochearnhead Perth 72 A3
Lochgelly Fife 73 E5
Lochgilphead Argyll 70 B6
Lochgoilhead Argyll 70 D4
Lochinver Suth 85 B5
Lochmaben Dumf 59 F3
Lochmaddy N. Uist 88 E1
Lochnagar, mt. A'deen 76 C3
Lochranza Arran 63 F3
Lochwinnoch Renf 64 B3
Lochy, Loch & R. I'ness 74 C3
Lockerbie Dumf 59 F3
Loddon Norf 39 G5
Loftus Yorks 55 F3
Logierait Perth 76 A5
Lomond Hills Fife 73 E4
Lomond, Loch Dunb/Stir 71 E5
London 19 F4
London Airport Middx 19 E4
London Colney Herts 19 F2
Long, Loch Argyll/Dunb 70 D5
Long Bennington Lincs 44 C6
Long Buckby Northants 28 B1
Long Compton Warks 27 G4
Long Crendon Bucks 18 B1
Long Eaton Derby 36 B1
Longforgan Perth 73 F2
Longformacus Berwick 66 D3
Longframlington N'land 61 F2
Longhorsley N'land 61 F2
Longhoughton N'land 61 G1
Long Itchington Warks 27 H1
Long Melford Suff 30 D3
Long Mynd, The Shrops 34 B5
Longniddry E. Loth 66 C1
Longnor Staffs 43 F4
Long Preston Yorks 48 B2
Longridge Lancs 47 F4
Longriggend Lanark 65 E2
Long Riston Yorks 51 F4
Long Sutton Lincs 37 H2
Longton Lancs 47 F5
Longton Staffs 35 E1
Longtown Cumb 60 A4
Looe, E. and W. Corn 3 G3
Loppington Shrops 34 B2
Lorne, Firth of Argyll 69 E6
Lossiemouth Moray 82 B1
Lostwithiel Corn 3 F2
Loudwater Bucks 18 D3
Loughborough Leics 36 B3
Loughor Glam 14 B2
Loughton Essex 19 H2
Louth Lincs 45 G3
Lowdham Notts 44 B6
Lowestoft Suff 39 H5
Loweswater W'land 52 B3
Lowick N'land 67 G4
Lowther Hills Lanark 59 E1
Loyal, Loch Suth 84 F3
Lubnaig, Loch Perth 72 A3
Ludford Magna Lincs 45 F3
Ludgershall Wilts 17 G6
Ludlow Shrops 26 A1
Luichart, Loch Ross 80 D2
Lulworth Cove Dorset 9 F6
Lumphanan A'deen 77 F1
Lunan B. Angus 77 F5
Lundin Links Fife 73 G4
Luss Dunb 71 E5
Lustleigh Devon 4 D3
Luton Beds 29 E5
Lutterworth Leics 36 B5
Lybster Caith 86 E4
Lydd & Airport Kent 13 F5
Lydford Devon 4 B2
Lydney Glos 16 B2
Lye Worcs 35 F5
Lyme Regis Dorset 5 H2
Lymington Hants 10 A5
Lymm Ches 42 C3
Lympne Kent 13 F3
Lyndhurst Hants 10 A4
Lyneham Wilts 17 E3
Lyneholme Ford Cumb 60 B4
Lynmouth Devon 7 E1
Lynton Devon 7 E1
Lytham St. Annes Lancs 46 D5
Mablethorpe Lincs 45 H3
Macclesfield Ches 43 E4
Macduff Banff 83 E1
Machrihanish Argyll 62 D5
Machynlleth Mont 33 E4
Madley Herefs 25 H4
Maenclochog Pemb 22 C3
Maes-teg Glam 14 D3
Maghull Lancs 42 A2
Magor Mon 15 H3
Maiden Bradley Wilts 9 E1
Maidenhead Berks 18 D3
Maiden Newton Dorset 8 D4
Maidstone Kent 12 D2
Malden Surrey 19 F5
Maldon Essex 20 D1
Mallaig I'ness 79 E8
Mallardoch, Loch Ross 80 C4
Malmesbury Wilts 16 D3
Malpas Ches 42 B6
Maltby Yorks 44 A2
Malton Yorks 50 C1
Malvern Hills Worcs 26 C4
Malvern Link Worcs 26 C3
Mam Soul, mt. I'ness 80 B5
Man, Isle of 46 A4
Manaccan Corn 2 C5
Manby Lincs 45 G3
Manchester Lancs 42 D1
Manningtree Essex 31 E5
Mansfield Notts 44 A5
Mansfield Woodhouse Notts 44 A4
Manston Kent 13 H1
Marazion Corn 2 B5
March Cambs 37 H5
Marden, N. and E. Sussex 11 E3
Maree, Loch Ross 80 A1
Margate Kent 13 H1
Marham Norf 38 C4
Market Bosworth Leics 36 A4
Market Deeping Lincs 37 F3
Market Drayton Shrops 34 D1
Market Harborough Leics 36 C5
Market Lavington Wilts 17 E5
Market Rasen Lincs 45 E2
Market Weighton Yorks 50 D4
Markinch Fife 73 F4
Marks Tey Essex 30 D5
Marlborough Wilts 17 F4
Marloes Pemb 22 A5
Marlow Bucks 18 C3
Marple Ches 43 E3
Marsden Yorks 43 E1
Marshfield Glos 16 C4
Marske Yorks 55 E5
Marston Green Warks 35 G5
Marston Montgomery Derby 35 G1
Marstow Herefs 26 B5
Martinhoe Devon 7 E1
Martlesham Suff 31 F3
Martley Worcs 26 C2
Martock Som 8 C3
Maryculter Kinc 77 H1
Marykirk Kinc 77 F4
Maryport Cumb 52 A2
Masham Yorks 49 E1
Massingham Norf 38 C2
Matlock Derby 43 G5
Mauchline Ayr 64 C5
Maud A'deen 83 G2
Maxton Rox 66 D5
Maxwelltown Kirkcud 59 E4
May, Isle of Fife 73 H4
Maybole Ayr 56 C3
Mayfield Sussex 12 C4
Meigle Perth 73 F1
Meikleour Perth 73 E1
Melbourn Cambs 29 G3
Melbourne Derby 36 A2
Melksham Wilts 16 D5
Melmerby Cumb 53 E2
Melness Suth 84 F2
Melrose Rox 66 C5
Meltham Yorks 43 F1
Melton Constable Norf 39 E2
Melton Mowbray Leics 36 C3
Melton Ross Lincs 45 E1
Melvaig Ross 78 E1
Melvich Suth 86 B2
Menai Bridge Angl 40 C4
Mendip Hills Som 16 A5
Menteith, L. of Perth 71 G4
Mere Ches 42 C3
Mere Wilts 9 E1
Merionethshire, co. 32 D2
Mersea I. Essex 31 E6
Mersey, R. Ches 42 A3
Merstham Surrey 19 G6
Merthyr Tydfil Glam 15 F1
Metheringham Lincs 45 E5
Methil Fife 73 F4
Methlick A'deen 83 G3
Methven Perth 72 D2
Methwold Norf 38 C5
Mevagissey Corn 3 E4
Mexborough Yorks 43 H1

Mey, Castle of — Rhiconich

Mey, Castle of *Caith* 86 F1
Meyllteyrn *Caern* 32 A2
Micklefield, New & Old *Yorks* 49 F5
Mickleton *Glos* 27 F3
Midcalder *M'loth* 65 G2
Middlebie *Dumf* 59 G4
Middleham *Yorks* 54 A6
Middlesbrough *Yorks* 54 D3
Middlesex, co. 19 E3
Middleton *Lancs* 42 D1
Middleton-in-Teesdale *Durham* 53 H2
Middleton-One-Row *Durham* 54 C4
Middleton Stoney *Oxon* 28 A5
Middle Wallop *Hants* 10 A1
Middlewich *Ches* 42 C4
Midhurst *Sussex* 11 E3
Midlothian, co. 65 G3
Midtown Brae *Ross* 78 F2
Milborne *Dorset* 9 E4
Milborne Port *Som* 9 E3
Mildenhall *Suff* 30 C1
Milford *Surrey* 11 F1
Milford Haven *Pemb* 22 B5
Milford-on-Sea *Hants* 10 A5
Millom *Cumb* 46 C1
Millport *Bute* 63 H2
Milnathort *Kinross* 73 E4
Milngavie *Dunb* 64 C2
Milnrow *Lancs* 43 E1
Milnthorpe *W'land* 47 F1
Milverton *Som* 8 A2
Minchinhampton *Glos* 16 D2
Minehead *Som* 7 G1
Mingulay, I. *I'ness* 88 D4
Mintlaw *A'deen* 83 H2
Mirfield *Yorks* 48 D6
Misterton *Notts* 44 C2
Mitcheldean *Glos* 26 B5
Modbury *Devon* 4 C5
Moffat *Dumf* 59 F1
Mold *Flint* 41 H5
Moniaive *Dumf* 58 D3
Monifieth *Angus* 73 G2
Monkhopton *Shrops* 34 C5
Monkton *Ayr* 64 B5
Monmouth *Mon* 16 A1
Monmouthshire, co. 15 G1
Montgomery *Mont* 33 H4
Montgomeryshire, co. 33 F4
Montrose *Angus* 77 G5
Monymusk *A'deen* 83 E5
Moorfoot Hills 66 B3
Morar *I'ness* 68 E1
Moray, co. 82 A2
Morden *Surrey* 19 F4
More, Loch *Suth* 84 D4
Morebattle *Rox* 67 E6
Morecambe *Lancs* 47 E2
Moreton Hampstead *Devon* 4 D2
Moreton-in-Marsh *Glos* 27 F4
Morley *Yorks* 49 E5
Morlich, Loch *I'ness* 81 H6
Morpeth *N'land* 61 F3
Morriston *Glam* 14 C2
Mortehoe *Devon* 6 D1
Mortimer's Cross *Herefs* 25 H2
Morvah *Corn* 2 A5
Morven *Argyll* 68 E3
Morven *Caith* 86 C4
Morville *Shrops* 34 D5
Mossley *Lancs* 43 E1
Mostyn *Flint* 41 G3
Motherwell *Lanark* 65 E3
Mottram *Ches* 43 E2
Mountain Ash *Glam* 15 F2
Mountsorrel *Leics* 36 B3
Mousehole *Corn* 2 A5
Mouswald *Dumf* 59 F4
Moy *I'ness* 75 E3
Moy *I'ness* 81 G4
Muchalls *Kinc* 77 H2
Much Birch *Herefs* 26 A4
Much Hadham *Herts* 29 H5
Much Wenlock *Shrops* 34 C4
Mucklestone *Staffs* 34 D1
Muirdrum *Angus* 71 H1
Muirkirk *Ayr* 56 F2
Muir-of-Ord *Ross* 81 E3
Mull, I. *Argyll* 69 D5
Mullion *Corn* 2 C6
Mull of Galloway *Wig* 57 B8
Mumbles *Glam* 14 C3
Mundesley *Norf* 39 G2
Mundford *Norf* 38 C5
Munlochy *Ross* 81 F2
Murthly *Perth* 72 D1
Musselburgh *M'loth* 66 B2
Muthill *Perth* 72 C3
Mybster *Caith* 86 E2
Nailsworth *Glos* 16 D2
Nairn *Nairn* 81 H2
Nairn, co. 81 G3
Nantgaredig *Carm* 23 F3
Nantwich *Ches* 42 C6
Narberth *Pemb* 22 D4
Naunton *Glos* 27 F5
Naver, Loch *Suth* 84 F4
Nayland *Suff* 30 D3
Neasham *Durham* 54 C4
Neath *Glam* 14 D2
Needham Market *Suff* 31 E3
Needles, The *I. of Wight* 10 A6
Nefyn *Caern* 32 B1
Nelson *Lancs* 47 H4
Ness, Loch *I'ness* 81 E5
Neston *Ches* 41 H4
Nether Stowey *Som* 8 A1
Netherton *Devon* 5 E3
Nether Wallop *Hants* 10 A1
Nethybridge *I'ness* 82 A5
Netley *Hants* 10 B4
Nettlebed *Oxon* 18 B3
New Abbey *Kirkcud* 59 E5
New Aberdour *A'deen* 83 G1
New Alresford *Hants* 10 C2
Newark *Notts* 44 C5
New Barnet *Herts* 19 F2
Newbiggin-by-the-Sea *N'land* 61 G3
Newborough *Angl* 40 B5
Newbridge *Corn* 3 H2
Newbridge *Mon* 15 G2
Newbridge-on-Wye *Radn* 25 E2
Newbrough *N'land* 60 D4
New Buckenham *Norf* 39 E5
Newburgh *A'deen* 83 H4
Newburgh *Fife* 73 F3
Newbury *Berks* 17 H5
Newby Bridge *Lancs* 52 D6
Newcastle Emlyn *Carm* 23 E2
Newcastleton *Rox* 60 B3
Newcastle-under-Lyme *Staffs* 42 D6
Newcastle-upon-Tyne *N'land* 61 G5
New Coylton *Ayr* 64 B6
New Cumnock *Ayr* 56 F3
New Dailly *Ayr* 56 C4
New Deer *A'deen* 83 G2
Newent *Glos* 26 C5
New Forest *Hants* 10 A4
New Galloway *Kirkcud* 58 C4
Newgate Sands *Pemb* 22 B4
Newhaven *Sussex* 12 B6
New Holland *Lincs* 51 E5
Newhouse *Lanark* 65 E3
New Hunstanton *Norf* 38 B1
Newlands Corner *Surrey* 19 E6
Newlyn *Corn* 2 A5
Newlyn East *Corn* 2 D3
Newmachar *A'deen* 83 G5
Newmarket *Suff* 30 B2
New Mills *Derby* 43 E3
Newmilns *Ayr* 64 C5
Newnham *Glos* 26 C6
New Pitsligo *A'deen* 83 G2
Newport *Essex* 30 A4
Newport *I. of Wight* 10 C5
Newport *Mon* 15 G3
Newport *Pemb* 22 C2
Newport *Shrops* 34 D3
Newport-on-Tay *Fife* 73 G2
Newport Pagnell *Bucks* 28 D3
New Quay *Card* 24 A2
Newquay *Corn* 2 D2
New Radnor *Radn* 25 G2
New Romney *Kent* 13 F4
New Scone *Perth* 73 E2
Newton *Dumf* 59 F2
Newton *Notts* 44 B6
Newton Abbot *Devon* 5 E3
Newtonferrers *Devon* 4 C5
Newtongrange *M'loth* 66 B2
Newton Heath *Lancs* 42 D2
Newton-le-Willows *Lancs* 42 B2
Newtonmore *I'ness* 75 G2
Newton-on-the-Moor *N'land* 61 F1
Newton Poppleford *Devon* 5 F2
Newton Stewart *Wig* 57 D6
Newtown *Mont* 33 H5
Newtown St. Boswells *Rox* 66 D5
Newtyle *Angus* 73 F1
Neyland *Pemb* 22 C5
Norfolk, co. 38 C3
Norham *N'land* 67 F4
Normanton *Yorks* 49 F5
Normanton-on-Trent *Notts* 44 C4
Northallerton *Yorks* 54 C4
Northampton *Northants* 28 C2
Northamptonshire, co. 28 B1
North Berwick *E. Loth* 66 C1
North Chapel *Sussex* 11 F2
North Downs *Kent/Surrey* 12 D1
Northfield *Warks* 35 F6
North Foreland *Kent* 13 H1
Northleach *Glos* 17 F1
North Luffenham *Rutl* 37 E4
North Molton *Devon* 7 E2
Northolt *Middx* 19 E3
Northop *Flint* 41 H4
North Riding, div. *Yorks* 54 B5
North Shields *N'land* 61 H4
North Tawton *Devon* 7 E5
North Uist, I. *I'ness* 88 D1
Northumberland, co. 60 D3
North Walsham *Norf* 39 G2
North Weald Bassett *Essex* 20 B2
Northwich *Ches* 42 C4
Northwood *Middx* 19 E3
Norton *Durham* 54 D3
Norwich *Norf* 39 F4
Nottingham *Notts* 36 B1
Nottinghamshire, co. 44 A5
Nuneaton *Warks* 36 A5
Oakengates *Shrops* 34 D3
Oakham *Rutl* 36 D3
Oakhill *Som* 16 B6
Oakington *Cambs* 29 H2
Oakley *Bucks* 18 B1
Oakworth *Yorks* 48 C4
Oban *Argyll* 70 B2
Ochil Hills 72 C4
Ochiltree *Ayr* 64 C6
Ockley *Surrey* 11 G1
Odiham *Hants* 18 C6
Oich, Loch *I'ness* 74 D2
Okehampton *Devon* 4 C2
Old Brompton *Derby* 43 H4
Oldbury *Worcs* 35 F5
Old Deer *A'deen* 83 G2
Oldham *Lancs* 43 E1
Old Kilpatrick *Dunb* 64 C2
Old Meldrum *A'deen* 83 F4
Old Sarum *Wilts* 9 H1
Old Shoreham *Sussex* 11 H4
Old Warden *Beds* 29 F3
Ollerton *Notts* 44 B4
Olney *Bucks* 28 D3
Ombersley *Worcs* 26 D2
Onchan *Isle of Man* 46 B5
Onich *I'ness* 74 B5
Orford *Suff* 31 G3
Orkney, Is. & co. 89
Ormiston *E. Loth* 66 B2
Ormskirk *Lancs* 42 A1
Oronsay, I. *Argyll* 69 C8
Orpington *Kent* 19 H5
Orrell Post *Lancs* 42 B1
Orton *W'land* 53 F4
Osbaldeston *Lancs* 47 G5
Osbournby *Lincs* 37 F1
Ossett *Yorks* 49 E5
Oswaldtwistle *Lancs* 47 G5
Oswestry *Shrops* 34 E2
Otford *Kent* 12 B1
Othery *Som* 8 B2
Otley *Yorks* 49 E4
Otterburn *N'land* 60 D2
Otter Ferry *Argyll* 70 B6
Ottershaw *Surrey* 19 E5
Otterton *Devon* 5 F2
Ottery St. Mary *Devon* 5 F2
Ottringham *Yorks* 51 G5
Oundle *Northants* 37 E5
Outwell *Cambs/Norf* 38 A4
Over *Ches* 42 C4
Overscaig *Suth* 85 D5
Overton *Flint* 34 B1
Over Whitacre *Warks* 35 H5
Ower *Hants* 10 A3
Oxford *Oxon* 18 A1
Oxfordshire, co. 27 G5
Oxshot *Surrey* 19 F5
Oykell Bridge *Suth* 85 D6
Padiham *Lancs* 47 H4
Padstow *Corn* 2 D1
Paignton *Devon* 5 E4
Painswick *Glos* 16 D1
Paisley *Renf* 64 C3
Pakefield *Suff* 39 H5
Pangbourne *Berks* 18 B4
Pannal *Yorks* 49 E3
Paps of Jura, mt. *Jura* 62 C1
Parkeston *Essex* 31 F5
Parkgate *Dumf* 59 E3
Pateley Bridge *Yorks* 48 D2
Pathhead *Fife* 73 F5
Pathhead *M'loth* 66 B2
Patna *Ayr* 56 D3
Patrington *Yorks* 51 G5
Patterdale *W'land* 52 D3
Peacehaven *Sussex* 12 A6
Peak, The, mt. *Derby* 43 F3
Peaslake *Surrey* 11 G1
Peebles *Peebl* 66 A4
Peeblesshire, co. 66 A6
Peel *Isle of Man* 46 A5
Pembrey *Glam* 14 A2
Pembridge *Herefs* 25 H2
Pembroke *Pemb* 22 C5
Pembroke Dock *Pemb* 22 C5
Pembrokeshire, co. 22 B3
Penarth *Glam* 15 G4
Pendlebury *Lancs* 42 D1
Penicuik *M'loth* 65 H3
Penistone *Yorks* 43 G1
Penkridge *Staffs* 35 F3
Penmaen-mawr *Caern* 40 D4
Penn *Bucks* 18 D2
Pennan *A'deen* 83 F1
Penrhyndeudraeth *Mer* 32 D1
Penrith *Cumb* 53 E2
Penruddock *Cumb* 52 D2
Penryn *Corn* 2 D5
Pensarn *Denb* 41 F3
Pentland Firth 89 A7
Pentland Hills 65 G3
Pentraeth *Angl* 40 C4
Pentrefoelas *Denb* 41 E6
Pen-y-groes *Caern* 40 B6
Penzance *Corn* 2 A5
Perranporth *Corn* 2 C3
Pershore *Worcs* 26 D3
Perth *Perth* 72 D2
Perthshire, co. 72 A1
Peterborough *Northants* 37 G4
Peterculter *A'deen* 77 G1
Peterhead *A'deen* 83 H2
Petersfield *Hants* 10 D3
Petworth *Sussex* 11 F3
Pewsey *Wilts* 17 F5
Pickering *Yorks* 55 F6
Pickering, Vale of *Yorks* 50 C2
Piercebridge *Durham* 53 B3
Pill *Som* 16 A4
Pinner *Middx* 19 E3
Pinwherry *Ayr* 56 C4
Pitchcombe *Glos* 16 D1
Pitlochry *Perth* 76 A5
Pittenweem *Fife* 73 H4
Plocton *Ross* 79 F5
Pluckley *Kent* 13 E3
Plymouth *Devon* 4 B5
Plympton *Devon* 4 C5
Plynlimonfawr, mt. *Card* 33 E5
Pocklington *Yorks* 50 C3
Polegate *Sussex* 12 C6
Pollokshaws *Lanark* 64 C3
Polmont *Stirl* 65 F1
Polperro *Corn* 3 G3
Polruan *Corn* 3 F3
Ponders End *Middx* 9 G2
Pontardawe *Glam* 23 H5
Pontefract *Yorks* 49 F5
Ponteland *N'land* 61 F4
Pont-erwyd *Card* 33 E6
Pontrhydfendigaid *Card* 24 C2
Pontrilas *Herefs* 25 H5
Pont-y-Berem *Carm* 23 F4
Pontypool *Mon* 15 G2
Pontypridd *Glam* 15 F3
Poole *Dorset* 9 G5
Poolewe *Ross* 78 F2
Porlock *Som* 7 F1
Port Appin *Argyll* 74 B6
Portaskaig *Islay* 62 B1
Port Carlisle *Cumb* 59 G5
Port Charlotte *Islay* 62 A2
Port Ellen *Islay* 62 B3
Portencross *Ayr* 64 A4
Port Erin *Isle of Man* 46 A6
Port Erroll *A'deen* 83 H3
Portessie *Banff* 82 D1
Port Eynon *Glam* 14 B3
Port Glasgow *Renf* 64 B2
Portgordon *Moray* 82 C1
Porthcawl *Glam* 14 D4
Porthleven *Corn* 2 C5
Portinscale *Cumb* 52 C3
Portishead *Som* 16 A4
Portknockie *Banff* 82 D1
Portland *Dorset* 9 E6
Portlethen *Kinc* 77 H2
Portmadoc *Caern* 32 D1
Portmahomack *Ross* 87 C7
Portnacroish *Argyll* 74 B6
Portnahaven *Islay* 62 A3
Portobello *M'loth* 66 B2
Port of Menteith *Perth* 72 A4
Port of Ness *Lewis* 88 C1
Portpatrick *Wig* 57 A7
Portreath *Corn* 2 C4
Portree *Skye* 79 C5
Port St. Mary *Isle of Man* 46 A6
Port Seton *E. Loth* 66 B1
Portskewett *Mon* 16 A3
Portsmouth *Hants* 10 D4
Port Sonachan *Argyll* 70 C3
Portsoy *Banff* 83 E1
Port Talbot *Glam* 14 D3
Port William *Wig* 57 D7
Postbridge *Devon* 4 C3
Potters Bar *Middx* 19 F2
Potton *Beds* 29 F3
Poulton-le-Fylde *Lancs* 47 E4
Praze-an-Beeble *Corn* 2 C5
Preesall *Lancs* 47 E3
Prendergast *Pemb* 22 C4
Prescot *Lancs* 42 A2
Prestatyn *Flint* 41 G3
Presteigne *Radn* 25 G2
Preston *Lancs* 47 F5
Preston Candover *Hants* 10 C1
Prestwich *Lancs* 42 D1
Prestwick *Ayr* 64 B6
Princes Risborough *Bucks* 18 C2
Princetown *Devon* 4 C3
Probus *Corn* 2 D3
Prudhoe *N'land* 61 F5
Puckeridge *Herts* 29 G5
Puddletown *Dorset* 9 E5
Pudsey *Yorks* 49 E5
Pulborough *Sussex* 11 F3
Pumpsaint *Carm* 24 C4
Purbeck, I. of *Dorset* 9 F6
Purfleet *Essex* 20 B4
Purley *Surrey* 19 G5
Purston Jaglin *Yorks* 49 F6
Putford E. and W. *Devon* 6 C4
Putsham *Som* 15 F6
Pwllheli *Caern* 32 B2
Quantock Hills *Som* 8 A1
Queensborough *Kent* 21 E4
Queensbury *Yorks* 48 D5
Queensferry, N. *Fife* 73 E6
Queensferry, S. *W. Loth* 73 E6
Quirang, mt. *Skye* 78 C3
Quoich, Loch *I'ness* 74 B2
Quoich Bridge *I'ness* 74 B2
Raasay, I. *I'ness* 79 D5
Radcliffe *Lancs* 42 D1
Radcliffe-on-Trent *Notts* 36 C1
Radlett *Herts* 19 F2
Radnor Forest *Radn* 25 F2
Radnorshire, co. 25 E2
Radstock *Som* 16 C5
Raglan *Mon* 15 H1
Ram *Carm* 24 B3
Ramasaig *Skye* 79 A5
Rampside *Lancs* 46 D2
Ramsbottom *Lancs* 47 H6
Ramsey *Hunts* 37 G5
Ramsey *Isle of Man* 46 C4
Ramsey I. *Pemb* 22 A3
Ramsgate *Kent* 13 H1
Rannoch, Loch *Perth* 75 F5
Rannoch, Moor of *Argyll-Perth* 75 E6
Ratho *M'loth* 65 G2
Ratlinghope *Shrops* 34 B4
Rattlesden *Suff* 30 D2
Rattray *Perth* 73 E1
Ravenglass *Cumb* 52 B5
Ravenscar *Yorks* 55 G4
Ravensthorpe *Yorks* 49 E6
Rawtenstall *Lancs* 47 H5
Rayleigh *Essex* 20 D3
Raynham *Norf* 38 D2
Reading *Berks* 18 C4
Reay *Caith* 86 C2
Redbourn *Herts* 19 E1
Redcar *Yorks* 55 E3
Redditch *Worcs* 27 E1
Redhill *Surrey* 19 G6
Redruth *Corn* 2 C4
Redwick *Glos* 16 B3
Reedham *Norf* 39 H4
Reepham *Norf* 39 E3
Reeth *Yorks* 54 A5
Reigate *Surrey* 19 F6
Reighton *Yorks* 51 F1
Rempstone *Notts* 36 B2
Renfrew *Renf* 64 C2
Renfrewshire, co. 64 B3
Renton *Dunb* 64 B1
Rest and be Thankful *Argyll* 70 D4
Reston *Berwick* 67 F3
Rhayader *Radn* 25 E2
Rhiconich *Suth* 84 C3

Symington Zetland

Symington *Ayr* 64 B5
Symington *Lanark* 65 F5
Sywell *Northants* 28 D1
Tadcaster *Yorks* 49 G4
Tadley *Hants* 18 B5
Tain *Ross* 87 B7
Talgarth *Brecon* 25 F4
Tal-sarnau *Mer* 32 D1
Talybont *Card* 32 D5
Tamworth *Staffs* 35 G4
Tangmere *Sussex* 11 E4
Tarbat Ness *Ross* 87 C7
Tarbert *Argyll* 63 E1
Tarbert *Harris* 88 B3
Tarbet *Dunb* 71 E4
Tarbolton *Ayr* 64 B6
Tarland *A'deen* 82 D6
Tarporley *Ches* 42 B5
Tattershall *Lincs* 45 F5
Taunton *Som* 8 A2
Taunton Deane, Vale of *Som* 8 A2
Tavistock *Devon* 4 B3
Tay, Loch *Perth* 72 A2
Tay, R. *Perth* 73 E3
Taynuilt *Argyll* 70 B2
Tayport *Fife* 73 G2
Tebay *W'land* 53 F4
Tedburn St. Mary *Devon* 4 D2
Teddington *Middx* 19 F4
Teignmouth *Devon* 5 E3
Templeton *Pemb* 22 D4
Tenbury *Shrops* 26 B1
Tenby *Pemb* 22 D5
Tendring *Essex* 31 E5
Tenterden *Kent* 13 E3
Ternhill *Shrops* 34 C2
Tetbury *Glos* 16 D2
Tetsworth *Oxon* 18 B2
Teversham *Cambs* 30 A2
Tewkesbury *Glos* 26 D4
Thame *Oxon* 18 C1
Thames Ditton *Surrey* 19 F5
Thanet, I. of *Kent* 13 H1
Thaxted *Essex* 30 B4
Theale *Berks* 18 B4
Thetford *Norf* 38 D6
Theydon Bois *Essex* 20 B2
Thirsk *Yorks* 49 F1
Thirston *N'land* 61 F2
Thornaby-on-Tees *Yorks* 54 D3
Thornbury *Glos* 16 B3
Thorne *Yorks* 50 C6
Thorney *Cambs* 37 G4
Thorney I. *Sussex* 10 D4
Thornhill *Dumf* 58 D2
Thornhill *Perth* 71 G4
Thornhill *Yorks* 49 E6
Thornton *Yorks* 48 D5
Thorpe-le-Soken *Essex* 31 F5
Thorpeness *Suff* 31 H2
Thorpe-on-the-Hill *Lincs* 44 D4
Thrapston *Northants* 37 E6
Threlkeld *Cumb* 52 C3
Threshfield *Yorks* 48 C2
Thruxton *Hants* 10 A1
Thurlow *Suff* 30 B3
Thursby *Cumb* 59 H6
Thurso *Caith* 86 D1
Tibberton *Shrops* 34 D3
Ticehurst *Sussex* 12 C4
Tickhill *Yorks* 44 B2
Tideswell *Derby* 43 F4
Tighnabruaich *Argyll* 63 F1
Tilbury *Essex* 20 C4
Tillicoultry *Clack* 72 C5
Tilshead *Wilts* 17 E6
Tintern Abbey *Mon* 16 A2
Tipton *Staffs* 35 F5
Tiptree *Essex* 30 D6
Tisbury *Wilts* 9 F2
Titchfield *Hants* 10 C4
Tiverton *Devon* 7 G4
Tobermory *Mull* 68 C3
Todmorden *Yorks* 48 C5
Tollerton *Notts* 36 C1
Tollesbury *Essex* 21 E1
Tolleshunt d'Arcy *Essex* 21 E1
Tomatin *I'ness* 81 G4
Tomdoun *I'ness* 74 C2
Tomintoul *Banff* 82 B5
Tonbridge *Kent* 12 C2
Tongue *Suth* 84 F2
Topcliffe *Yorks* 49 F1
Topsham *Devon* 5 F2
Torcross *Devon* 5 E6
Torpoint *Corn* 3 H3
Torquay *Devon* 5 E4
Torrance *Stirl* 64 D2
Torridon *Ross* 80 A2
Torver *W'land* 52 C5
Totland *I. of Wight* 10 A5
Totley *Yorks* 43 G3
Totnes *Devon* 5 E4
Tottenham *Middx* 19 G3
Totton *Hants* 10 B3
Towcester *Northants* 28 C3
Tow Law *Durham* 54 A1
Towyn *Mer* 32 D4
Tranent *E. Loth* 66 B2
Traquair *Peebl* 66 B5
Tredegar *Mon* 15 F1
Treforest *Glam* 15 F3
Tregaron *Cardigan* 24 C2
Tregony *Corn* 3 E4
Treharris *Glam* 15 F2
Trelleck *Mon* 16 A1
Treorchy *Glam* 15 E2
Tresparrett Posts *Corn* 6 A5
Trimdon *Durham* 54 C2
Trimley *Suff* 31 F4
Tring *Herts* 18 D1
Troon *Ayr* 64 B5
Trossachs, The *Perth* 71 F4
Trowbridge *Wilts* 16 D4
Trumpington *Cambs* 29 H2
Truro *Corn* 2 D4
Tugby *Leics* 36 D4
Tulloch *I'ness* 75 E3
Tumby *Lincs* 45 F5
Tummel, Loch *Perth* 75 H5
Tummel Bridge *Perth* 75 G5
Tunbridge Wells, Royal *Kent* 12 C3
Tunstall *Staffs* 42 D5
Turnberry *Ayr* 56 C3
Turnditch *Derby* 43 G6
Turnershill *Sussex* 11 H2
Turriff *A'deen* 83 F2
Tutbury *Staffs* 35 H2
Tuxford *Notts* 44 C4
Tweed, R. 67 F3
Tweedmouth *N'land* 67 F3
Tweedsmuir *Peebl* 65 G6
Twickenham *Middx* 19 F4
Two Bridges *Devon* 4 C3
Twycross *Leics* 36 A4
Twyford *Berks* 18 C4
Twyford *Bucks* 28 B5
Twyford *Hants* 10 B3
Twynholm *Kirkcud* 58 C6
Tyldesley *Lancs* 42 C1
Tyndrum *Perth* 71 E2
Tyne, R. *N'land* 61 G5
Tynemouth *N'land* 61 H4
Tyn-y-Groes *Caern* 40 D4
Uckfield *Sussex* 12 B4
Uddingston *Lanark* 64 D3
Uffculme *Devon* 7 H4
Uig *Lewis* 88 A2
Uig *Skye* 78 B3
Ulceby *Lincs* 51 E6
Ulceby Cross *Lincs* 45 G4
Uldale *Cumb* 52 C2
Ullapool *Ross* 85 B7
Ullswater *Cumb-W'land* 52 D3
Ulva, I. *Argyll* 68 C4
Ulverston *Lancs* 46 D1
Unapool *Suth* 84 C4
Unst, I. *Shet* 89 F5
Uny Lelant *Corn* 2 B4
Upavon *Wilts* 17 F5
Uphall *W. Loth* 65 G2
Upham *Hants* 10 C3
Upholland *Lancs* 42 B1
Upper Tean *Staffs* 35 F1
Uppingham *Rutl* 36 D4
Upton-upon-Severn *Worcs* 26 D4
Urmston *Lancs* 42 D2
Urquhart *Moray* 82 C1
Usk *Mon* 15 H2
Uttoxeter *Staffs* 35 G1
Uxbridge *Middx* 19 E3
Valley *Angl* 40 A3
Vatersay, I. *I'ness* 88 D4
Venachar, Loch *Perth* 71 G4
Ventnor *I. of Wight* 10 C6
Virginia Water *Surrey* 18 D4
Voil, Loch *Perth* 71 F3
Vyrnwy, L. *Mont* 33 F2
Waddesdon *Bucks* 28 C5
Waddington *Lincs* 44 D4
Wadebridge *Corn* 3 E1
Wadhurst *Sussex* 12 C4
Wainfleet *Lincs* 45 H5
Wakefield *Yorks* 49 E6
Wakes Colne *Essex* 30 D5
Walford *Herefs* 25 H1
Walkden *Lancs* 42 C1
Walkerburn *Peebl* 66 B5
Wallasey *Ches* 41 H2
Wallingford *Berks* 18 B3
Walls *Shet* 89 D7
Wallsend *N'land* 61 G4
Walmer *Kent* 13 H2
Walney I. *Lancs* 46 C2
Walsall *Staffs* 35 F4
Walsall Wood *Staffs* 35 F4
Walsingham *Norf* 38 D1
Waltham Abbey *Essex* 19 G2
Waltham Cross *Herts* 19 G2
Waltham-on-the-Wolds *Leics* 19 F5
Walthamstow *Essex* 19 G3
Walton *Cumb* 60 B5
Walton-on-Thames *Surrey* 19 E5
Walton-on-the-Hill *Surrey* 19 F5
Walton-on-the-Naze *Essex* 31 F6
Wangford *Suff* 31 H1
Wanlockhead *Dumf* 58 D1
Wanstead *Essex* 19 G3
Wantage *Berks* 17 G3
Warboys *Hunts* 37 G6
Wardington *Oxon* 27 H3
Ware *Herts* 19 G1
Wareham *Dorset* 9 F5
Wargrave *Berks* 18 C4
Wark *N'land* 60 D4
Warkworth *N'land* 61 G1
Warlingham *Surrey* 12 A1
Warminster *Wilts* 16 D6
Warnham *Sussex* 11 G2
Warrington *Lancs* 42 B3
Warsop *Notts* 44 B3
Warton *Lancs* 47 E5
Warwick *Cumb* 60 A5
Warwick *Warks* 27 G2
Warwickshire, co. 27 F1
Wash, The 38 A1
Washington *Durham* 61 G5
Washington *Sussex* 11 G4
Wast Water *Cumb* 52 B4
Watchet *Som* 7 H1
Waterbeach *Cambs* 30 A2
Watford *Herts* 19 E2
Watling Street *Northants* 28 C3
Watlington *Oxon* 18 B2
Watten *Caith* 86 E2
Watton *Norf* 38 D4
Watton-at-Stone *Herts* 29 G5
Wealdstone *Middx* 19 F3
Wednesbury *Staffs* 35 F5
Wednesfield *Staffs* 35 F4
Weedon Beck *Northants* 28 B2
Week St. Mary *Corn* 6 B5
Weeley *Essex* 31 E5
Welbeck Abbey *Notts* 44 A4
Welford *Northants* 36 C6
Wellingborough *Northants* 28 D1
Wellington *Shrops* 34 D3
Wellington *Som* 8 A2
Wells *Norf* 38 D1
Wells *Som* 16 B6
Welshampton *Shrops* 34 B1
Welshpool *Mont* 33 H4
Welwyn *Herts* 29 F6
Welwyn Garden City *Herts* 19 F1
Wem *Shrops* 34 C2
Wembley *Middx* 19 F3
Wemyss Bay *Argyll* 63 H1
Wendover *Bucks* 18 D1
Wendron *Corn* 2 C5
Wenlock Edge *Shrops* 34 B5
Wenvoe *Glam* 15 F4
Wensleydale *Yorks* 54 A5
Weobley *Herefs* 25 H3
West Auckland *Durham* 54 B2
West Bridgford *Notts* 36 B1
West Bromwich *Staffs* 35 F5
Westbury *Wilts* 16 D6
Westbury-upon-Severn *Glos* 26 C6
West Calder *M'loth* 65 G3
Westerham *Kent* 12 B2
Westgate-on-Sea *Kent* 13 H1
West Gordon *Berwick* 66 D4
West Haddon *Northants* 28 B1
West Ham *Essex* 20 A3
West Hartlepool *Durham* 54 D2
West Kilbride *Ayr* 64 A4
West Kirby *Ches* 41 G3
West Linton *Peebl* 65 G3
West Meon *Hants* 10 D3
West Mersea *Essex* 21 F1
Westmorland, co. 52 D4
Weston-super-Mare *Som* 15 G5
Westray, I. *Orkney* 89 B5
West Riding, div. *Yorks* 48 D4
Westruther *Berwick* 66 D3
West Thurrock *Essex* 20 C4
Westward Ho *Devon* 6 C2
West Wycombe *Middx* 18 C2
Wetherby *Yorks* 49 F3
Wetwang *Yorks* 50 D3
Weybridge *Surrey* 19 E5
Weyhill *Hants* 10 A1
Weymouth *Dorset* 9 E6
Whaley Bridge *Derby* 43 E3
Whalley *Lancs* 47 G4
Whalsay, I. *Shet* 89 F7
Whalton *N'land* 61 F3
Wharfedale *Yorks* 48 D3
Wheathampstead *Herts* 19 F1
Wheatley *Oxon* 18 B1
Whickham *Durham* 61 G5
Whiddon Down *Devon* 4 D2
Whimple *Devon* 5 F1
Whipsnade *Beds* 29 E6
Whitburn *Durham* 61 H5
Whitburn *W. Loth* 65 F2
Whitby *Yorks* 55 G4
Whitchurch *Bucks* 28 C5
Whitchurch *Glam* 15 F3
Whitchurch *Hants* 10 B1
Whitchurch *Herefs* 26 B5
Whitchurch *Shrops* 34 C1
Whitehaven *Cumb* 52 A3
Whitehills *Banff* 83 E1
White Horse, Vale of *Berks* 17 G2
Whitekirk *E. Loth* 66 D1
Whiteparish *Wilts* 10 A3
White Waltham *Berks* 18 D4
Whithorn *Wig* 57 E8
Whiting Bay *Arran* 63 G5
Whitland *Carm* 22 D4
Whitletts *Ayr* 64 B6
Whitley *Yorks* 49 E6
Whitley Bay *N'land* 61 H4
Whitstable *Kent* 13 F1
Whittingham *N'land* 60 F1
Whittington *Shrops* 34 A2
Whittlesey *Cambs* 37 G4
Whitton *Radn* 25 G2
Whitwell *I. of Wight* 10 C6
Whitworth *Lancs* 48 B6
Wick *Caith* 86 F3
Wickford *Essex* 20 D2
Wickham *Hants* 10 C4
Wickham Market *Suff* 31 G3
Wickwar *Glos* 16 C3
Widecombe-in-the-Moor *Devon* 4 D3
Widmerpool *Notts* 36 C2
Widnes *Lancs* 42 B3
Wigan *Lancs* 42 B1
Wigginton *Yorks* 49 G2
Wight, Isle of *Hants* 10 B6
Wigmore *Herefs* 25 H1
Wigston Magna *Leics* 36 C4
Wigton *Cumb* 52 C1
Wigtown *Wig* 57 E7
Wigtownshire, co. 57 B6
Wilburton *Cambs* 29 H1
Willenhall *Staffs* 35 F4
Willersley *Herefs* 25 G3
Willesden *Middx* 19 F3
Willingham *Cambs* 29 H1
Willington *Derby* 35 H2
Willington *Durham* 54 B2
Williton *Som* 7 H1
Wilmington *Kent* 20 B4
Wilmslow *Ches* 42 D3
Wilton *Wilts* 9 G2
Wiltshire, co. 16 D5
Wimbledon *Surrey* 19 F4
Wimborne Minster *Dorset* 9 G4
Wincanton *Som* 9 E2
Winchburgh *W. Loth* 65 G2
Winchcombe *Glos* 27 E4
Winchelsea *Sussex* 13 E5
Winchester *Hants* 10 C2
Windermere *W'land* 52 D5
Windsor *Berks* 18 D4
Windsor Great Park *Berks* 18 D4
Windygates *Fife* 73 F4
Winfrith Heath *Dorset* 9 E5
Wingham *Kent* 13 G2
Winnersh *Berks* 18 C4
Winscales *W'land* 52 A4
Winsford *Ches* 42 C4
Winslow *Bucks* 28 C5
Winster *Derby* 43 G5
Winterbourne Stoke *Wilts* 9 G1
Winteringham *Lincs* 50 D5
Winterton *Lincs* 50 D6
Winterton *Norf* 39 H3
Wirksworth *Derby* 43 G5
Wirral Pen. *Ches* 41 H3
Wisbech *Cambs* 37 H3
Wisborough Green *Sussex* 11 F3
Wishaw *Lanark* 65 E3
Witchampton *Dorset* 9 G4
Witham *Essex* 21 E1
Witheridge *Devon* 7 F4
Withern *Lincs* 45 H3
Withernsea *Yorks* 51 G5
Withington *Glos* 27 E6
Withington *Herefs* 26 B3
Withington *Lancs* 42 D2
Witley *Surrey* 11 F1
Witney *Oxon* 17 G1
Wittering *Northants* 37 F4
Wittering, E. and W. *Sussex* 11 E5
Witton-le-Wear *Durham* 54 B2
Wiveliscombe *Som* 7 H2
Wivenhoe *Essex* 31 E5
Woburn Sands *Beds-Bucks* 28 D4
Woking *Surrey* 19 E5
Wokingham *Berks* 18 C4
Wolsingham *Durham* 54 A2
Wolston *Warks* 27 H1
Wolverhampton *Staffs* 35 E4
Wolverton *Bucks* 28 C4
Wolvey *Warks* 36 A5
Wolviston *Durham* 54 D3
Wombwell *Yorks* 43 H1
Womersley *Yorks* 49 G6
Wonersh *Surrey* 19 E6
Woodbridge *Suff* 31 G3
Woodchester *Glos* 16 D2
Woodchurch *Kent* 13 E3
Wood End *Warks* 27 F1
Woodford *Essex* 20 B3
Woodford Halse *Northants* 28 B3
Woodhall Spa *Lincs* 45 F5
Woodhead *Ches* 43 F2
Woodstock *Oxon* 27 H5
Woofferton *Shrops* 26 A1
Woolacombe *Devon* 6 C1
Wooler *N'land* 67 F5
Woolton *Lancs* 42 A3
Woolwich *London* 19 H4
Woore *Shrops* 42 C6
Wootton Bassett *Wilts* 17 E3
Wootton Glanville *Dorset* 9 E3
Worcester *Worcs* 26 D2
Worcestershire, co. 26 C2
Workington *Cumb* 52 A2
Worksop *Notts* 44 B3
Worlds End *Warks* 35 F5
Worle *Som* 15 H5
Worlingham *Suff* 39 H5
Wormit *Fife* 73 G2
Worthing *Sussex* 11 G4
Wotton-under-Edge *Glos* 16 C2
Wragby *Lincs* 45 E3
Wragby *Yorks* 49 F6
Wrath, C. *Suth* 84 C1
Wrekin, The, mt. *Shrops* 34 C3
Wrentham *Suff* 31 H1
Wrexham *Denb* 42 A6
Wrightington *Lancs* 47 F6
Writtle *Essex* 20 C1
Wrotham *Kent* 12 C1
Wroughton *Wilts* 17 F3
Wroxham *Norfolk* 39 G3
Wye *Kent* 13 F2
Wyke Regis *Dorset* 8 D6
Wylye *Wilts* 9 G1
Wymeswold *Leics* 36 B2
Wymondham *Norf* 39 E4
Yapton *Sussex* 11 F4
Yardley *Warks* 35 G5
Yardley Chase *Northants* 28 D2
Yarm *Yorks* 54 C3
Yarmouth *I. of Wight* 10 B5
Yarrow Church *Selk* 66 B5
Yatton *Som* 16 A5
Yeadon *Yorks* 49 E4
Yealmpton *Devon* 4 C5
Yell, I. *Shet* 89 E6
Yelverton *Devon* 4 B4
Yeovil *Som* 8 D3
Yiewsley *Middx* 19 E3
York *Yorks* 49 G3
Yorkshire, co. 48 D1
Youlgreave *Derby* 44 G4
Yoxall *Staffs* 35 G3
Yoxford *Suff* 31 G2
Ystalyfera *Glam* 14 D1
Ystradgynlais *Brecon* 24 D6
Ystrad Mynach *Glam* 15 F2
Ystrad Rhondda *Glam* 15 E2
Zennor *Corn* 2 A4
Zetland, co. 89

The distance between any two towns listed here, can be found in the box formed at the junction of the vertical and horizontal rows reading from the names of the towns; e.g. to find the distance between Edinburgh and London, read down the vertical row from Edinburgh and along the horizontal row from London and the figure 373 will be found.

In general the distances are based on the shortest routes by classified roads.

	Aberdeen	Aberystwyth	Ayr	Birmingham	Bradford	Bristol	Cambridge	Cardiff	Carlisle	Coventry	Derby	Doncaster	Dover	Edinburgh	Exeter	Fishguard	Fort William	Glasgow	Gloucester	Harwich	Holyhead	Hull	Inverness	Kendal	Leeds	Leicester	Lincoln	Liverpool	Manchester	Newcastle-u	Norwich
Aberystwyth	427																														
Ayr	175	309																													
Birmingham	403	114	285																												
Bradford	318	197	200	108																											
Bristol	480	121	362	88	188																										
Cambridge	443	211	346	100	152	148																									
Cardiff	484	100	366	102	202	44	174																								
Carlisle	208	219	90	195	110	272	256	276																							
Coventry	417	132	299	18	114	91	81	114	209																						
Derby	384	138	266	40	74	127	96	142	176	40																					
Doncaster	326	172	229	93	34	181	117	195	139	92	54																				
Dover	552	284	455	181	260	187	112	226	365	163	52	226																			
Edinburgh	115	312	73	288	194	365	327	369	93	303	263	211	436																		
Exeter	555	196	437	163	266	75	218	119	347	167	203	256	243	440																	
Fishguard	482	56	364	167	216	146	263	112	274	185	194	228	322	367	221																
Fort William	152	416	132	392	307	469	453	473	197	406	373	336	561	130	544	471															
Glasgow	142	313	33	289	204	366	350	370	94	303	270	234	459	44	441	368	103														
Gloucester	448	107	330	53	156	35	117	56	240	57	93	146	176	333	110	145	437	334													
Harwich	509	271	413	159	220	188	66	228	323	141	163	183	112	393	242	317	519	417	172												
Holyhead	423	108	305	149	157	208	244	193	215	167	157	171	330	308	283	159	412	309	181	308											
Hull	337	214	240	123	64	203	123	224	150	111	88	42	232	222	278	270	347	245	168	185	214										
Inverness	104	468	198	444	350	521	484	525	249	459	419	367	593	156	596	523	66	169	489	550	464	378									
Kendal	253	174	135	150	65	227	215	231	45	164	131	99	324	138	302	229	242	139	195	282	170	124	294								
Leeds	306	166	206	109	9	194	144	209	116	110	70	28	253	191	269	221	313	210	159	211	163	55	347	71							
Leicester	412	153	295	39	100	116	68	137	205	24	28	69	169	280	191	206	402	299	81	135	178	87	436	160	96						
Lincoln	365	190	268	86	74	166	86	188	178	74	52	39	195	250	241	245	375	272	131	148	201	37	406	138	67	51					
Liverpool	327	100	208	90	66	159	174	164	118	107	81	86	268	211	235	156	315	213	128	241	97	128	368	73	73	107	118				
Manchester	326	126	208	80	34	159	154	172	118	94	59	51	255	211	236	181	315	221	126	221	123	93	367	73	40	87	84	35			
Newcastle-u	221	254	144	201	97	285	229	299	57	202	161	112	338	106	360	309	236	143	250	295	250	117	262	85	92	181	151	154	129		
Norwich	471	270	374	156	178	208	62	236	284	138	139	145	153	356	277	325	481	378	179	66	296	143	512	244	173	118	106	215	184	257	
	370	154	272	50	74	138	84	153	182	48	16	44	193	255	213	209	379	276	103	151	172	73	411	137	67	25	36	97	70	156	124
	464	156	347	64	165	69	80	105	257	50	90	138	129	348	138	194	454	352	49	125	210	156	505	212	160	69	119	154	142	250	139
	663	304	545	271	374	184	329	227	455	275	311	364	355	548	112	330	652	549	218	354	391	386	704	410	378	299	350	343	344	468	389
	81	353	94	330	235	406	369	411	135	345	305	253	478	42	482	409	103	61	375	436	350	264	115	180	233	322	291	253	252	148	397
	597	238	479	205	308	118	260	161	389	209	245	298	285	482	42	264	586	483	152	284	325	320	638	344	312	233	284	277	278	402	319
	543	211	425	141	242	92	126	136	335	127	167	215	125	426	123	238	532	429	104	144	282	233	583	290	237	146	196	228	219	327	183
	515	173	397	112	220	52	132	96	307	105	145	196	157	400	88	198	504	401	69	156	249	215	556	262	215	128	178	196	192	306	192
	338	154	235	77	37	164	116	179	145	78	37	18	225	223	240	209	342	240	130	183	158	61	379	100	33	62	46	73	38	124	145
	378	75	260	43	99	102	138	106	170	61	64	98	224	263	177	130	367	264	75	202	106	140	419	125	106	75	115	58	66	195	195
	528	195	412	128	227	75	129	118	322	114	154	202	139	413	105	221	519	416	91	149	269	220	569	277	224	133	184	216	207	314	189
	503	252	406	150	212	156	60	194	316	132	163	175	68	388	210	290	513	410	145	59	299	183	542	294	207	128	146	237	214	289	98
	362	109	244	43	69	124	123	138	154	57	34	65	219	247	199	164	351	248	89	190	123	107	403	109	73	55	85	51	37	164	173
	226	320	51	296	211	373	357	377	101	310	277	240	466	123	448	375	183	84	341	424	316	251	249	146	217	306	279	219	219	155	395
	226	590	315	565	472	643	606	647	371	581	541	489	715	278	718	645	183	285	611	672	586	500	122	416	569	558	528	490	489	384	634
	423	101	305	26	128	60	115	75	215	44	65	117	185	308	136	148	412	309	25	181	155	165	460	170	132	64	112	102	100	225	176
	299	190	203	127	33	215	151	229	113	126	88	34	260	184	290	245	314	207	180	217	187	38	340	86	24	103	73	97	64	81	179
	488	212	390	110	195	116	54	154	300	92	123	162	72	373	170	250	497	394	105	73	259	168	529	255	190	98	132	197	184	274	111